GOOD
AND
CHEAP

EAT WELL ON $4/DAY

GOOD

AND

CHEAP

LEANNE BROWN

WORKMAN PUBLISHING • NEW YORK

Library of Congress Cataloging-in-Publication Data is available.

ISBN 978-0-7611-8499-7

Design by Janet Vicario; layout by Gordon Whiteside
Cover photo by Leanne Brown
Additional Photo Credits: page 16 (from top to bottom): pixelrobot/fotolia, lester120/fotolia, arinahabich/fotolia, komodoempire/fotolia, simmittorok/fotolia, taiftin/fotolia; page 17 (from top to bottom): Tarzhanova/fotolia, Workman Publishing, Viktor/fotolia, photos777/fotolia, pioneer/fotolia, Andy Lidstone/fotolia.

Workman books are available at special discounts when purchased in bulk for premiums and sales promotions as well as for fund-raising or educational use. Special editions or book excerpts also can be created to specification. For details, contact the Special Sales Director at the address below, or send an email to specialmarkets@workman.com.

Workman Publishing Co., Inc.
225 Varick Street
New York, NY 10014-4381
workman.com

WORKMAN is a registered trademark of Workman Publishing Co., Inc.

Printed and bound in China/Partly sponsored by Asia Pacific Inc.
First printing June 2015

10 9 8 7 6 5

CONTENTS

INTRODUCTION

Eating is one of life's greatest pleasures. In a perfect world, healthy and delicious food would be all around us. It would be easy to choose and easy to enjoy.

But of course, it's not a perfect world. There are thousands of barriers that can keep us from eating in a way that nourishes our bodies and satisfies our tastes. Money just shouldn't be one of them.

Kitchen skill, not budget, is the key to great food. This cookbook is a celebration of the many delicious meals available to those on even the strictest of budgets.

Eating on a limited budget is not easy, and there are times when a tough week can turn mealtime into a chore. As one woman told me, "I'm weary of the 'what's for dinner?' game." I hope the recipes and techniques in this book can help make those times rare and the tough choices a little more bearable.

At the same time, this book is not a meal plan—those are much too individual to share on a wide scale. Every person and every family has specific needs and unique tastes. We live in different regions, different neighborhoods, and with varying means. One book cannot account for all of that, but I hope it can be a spark, a general strategy, a flexible set of approachable and cheap recipes. The rest is up to you.

I think you'll find (or perhaps have already found) that learning to cook has a powerfully positive effect. **If you can become a more skilled, more conscious cook, then you'll be able to conjure deliciousness in any kitchen, anytime.** Good cooking alone can't solve hunger in America, but it can make life happier—and that is worth every effort.

Just as a good meal is best shared with others, so is a good recipe. I may not be able to share a meal with you, but I'd love to offer a few ideas. **What's for dinner? Here's my answer.**

About This Book I created an earlier version of this book as the capstone project for my master's degree in food studies at New York University. After I posted a free PDF on my website (leannebrown.com), it went viral on Reddit, Tumblr, and elsewhere, racking up almost 100,000 downloads in the first few weeks. That support gave me the courage to launch a Kickstarter campaign to get printed copies of *Good and Cheap* into the hands of people who don't have computers or who wouldn't otherwise see it. Thousands of generous supporters contributed to the campaign, donating more than 9,000 free copies of the printed book and sponsoring twenty new recipes. That first printed edition of the book was self-published, and sold out within a few months. The PDF was downloaded about 500,000 times within six months after it was first posted. What you hold in your hands is a second edition, including 30 new recipes. The experience changed my life. I hope this book changes yours.

My Philosophy The best health advice is simple: Eat fruits and vegetables. Many American cookbooks rely on meat as the central feature of a meal. **My recipes celebrate the vegetables rather than the meat.** My intent was to create satisfying food that doesn't require you to supplement your meals with cheap carbohydrates to stave off hunger. **I strove to create recipes that use money carefully, without being purely slavish to the bottom line.** For example, many recipes use butter rather than oil. Butter is not cheap, but it creates flavor, crunch, and richness in a way that cheap oils never can.

I'm not a dietitian, and this isn't a diet book. I'm just a home cook, like you. If you have dietary restrictions, some recipes won't work for you as written, but that's fine—you can adapt them to your needs, or just turn the page and keep looking for inspiration.

More than a book of recipes, this is a book of ideas. I want you to tailor things to your taste. Improvisation is the soul of great cooking! If it doesn't work out every time, I hope you'll forgive me. More important, forgive yourself, and try again.

A NOTE ON $4/DAY

I designed these recipes to fit the budgets of people living on SNAP, the US federal program that used to be called food stamps. If you're on SNAP, you already know that the benefit formulas are complicated, but the rule of thumb is that you end up with $4 per person, per day, to spend on food.

This book isn't challenging you to live on so little—it's a resource in case that's your reality. In May 2014, there were 46 million Americans on food stamps. Untold millions more—in particular, retirees and students—live under similar constraints.

If you're in Canada, or anywhere else outside the United States, it might seem like this book won't apply to you. While the specifics may differ, learning to cook and take joy in simple, real food is great for anyone, anywhere.

The costs for each recipe are based on two sources. For the list of grocery ideas on page xiii, I collected prices from four grocery stores in a diverse neighborhood in New York. For specific spices and a wider variety of fruits and vegetables, I looked at online grocery stores or nationwide averages collected by the Bureau of Labor Statistics. The prices for fruits and vegetables assume that they're roughly in season, when you can get the best deals. This means, unfortunately, that you'll pay a lot more if you want to make peach coffee cake in February. I talk more about shopping in season on the following pages.

The estimates are, by necessity, a snapshot of place and time. Costs will vary in other cities, other neighborhoods, even just other stores. Please think of the numbers as a guideline, not a guarantee.

More than in most cookbooks, my recipes are flexible and encourage substitution based on availability, price, and personal tastes. A strict budget requires flexibility and a willingness to say, "That's a good deal this week, so it's what I'll be cooking!" Don't worry, you'll pick up the tricks quickly.

A few recipes call for fancy kitchen equipment, but in my work with low-income families in New York, I've found that items like blenders, food processors, and electric mixers are fairly common. I did not, however, attempt to tackle the very real situation of people who have no kitchen, no equipment, and no space to prepare food. I simply cannot hope to do those issues justice within the bounds of one cookbook. Let's all agree that we need to keep striving to address all the issues that make it difficult for so many people to eat well.

TIPS FOR EATING AND SHOPPING WELL

1 BUY FOODS THAT CAN BE USED IN MULTIPLE MEALS

Versatile ingredients save meals. If you buy flour, you can make Tortillas (page 155), Roti (page 152), Scones (page 15), and Pancakes (page 12). If you buy canned tomatoes, you can make soup (page 28), sauce (page 127), even chili (page 131). Need I even mention the versatility of garlic or lemons? If you always keep them around, you can make anything else taste fantastic.

2 BUY IN BULK

Buying larger amounts of one item can usually bring down the price per unit. When you're working within a tight budget, you won't always be able to afford to shop for the future, but you should do it when you can. And, of course, keep storage in mind: If the item will go bad before you can finish it, get the smaller size. Only buy what you can eat. If you buy versatile ingredients in slightly larger amounts, then you'll be able to use them quickly but still make diverse meals.

3 START BUILDING A PANTRY

If possible—and admittedly this can be difficult for people living on their own—reserve part of your budget to buy one or two semi-expensive pantry items each week or month. Things like olive oil, soy sauce, and spices (page 149) are pricey at first, but if you use just a little with each recipe, they go a long way. With turmeric, coriander, cumin, and chili powder, you'll suddenly have a world of flavor on your shelf. For specific advice, see page 149.

4 THINK WEEKLY

Each week, mix things up by buying different varieties of staple foods like grains and beans. This week, you might have Oatmeal every morning (page 9) with Dark and Spicy Chili (page 131) later in the day, but next week you'll have yogurt for breakfast (page xi) and Hummus (page 135) or Chana Masala (page 109) for lunch and dinner. If you have time to shop frequently, pick up smaller amounts of produce every couple of days to ensure everything is fresh. It's a lot more inspiring to pull crisp greens out of the fridge than to unstick a wilted mess from the bottom of the veggie drawer. If you can't shop as often, consider getting canned or frozen versions of the vegetables you won't use immediately.

5 THINK SEASONALLY

During their local growing season, fruits and vegetables are generally cheaper and definitely tastier than outside of season. You'll notice that orange prices shoot up during the summer, yet what's available is drab and flavorless. But oranges are abundant in December and January, the peak of their season, and that's reflected in the price. At the end of summer, you can get bags of zucchini for next to nothing. Brussels sprouts are also very seasonal, coming on sale around Thanksgiving. Enjoy as much of the summer and fall produce as possible, because you'll be more limited in the winter. Then again, simmering and roasting winter vegetables is a fine way to warm up your house, and tough winter roots are easy to store. In addition, winter is a great time to search for deals on canned and frozen produce. Seasons for fruits and vegetables vary depending on where you live, so consult a local guide to growing seasons (or the chart on page xv) and use it to shop for the best deals.

6 MORE VEGETABLES = MORE FLAVOR

Nothing livens up a bowl of rice like summer squash and corn! Vegetables make the best sauces: They're earthy, bright, tart, sweet, bitter, and savory. Give them a treasured spot at the top of your grocery list and you'll never be bored.

7 ALWAYS BUY EGGS

With these babies in your fridge, you're only minutes away from a satisfying meal. Scramble an egg with leftovers or drop an egg on top of a salad or a plate of stir-fried vegetables, and deliciousness is guaranteed.

8 BUY EXPENSIVE EGGS IF YOU CAN

Free-range or organic eggs are usually worth the money—they taste so much better than regular eggs. Even at $4 a dozen, you're still only paying 33 cents per egg. Really fresh eggs, like those from a farmers' market, make a big difference in flavor.

9 BE CAREFUL WITH UNDERCOOKED EGGS

Very rarely, raw eggs can be infected with salmonella. Many classic recipes, from mayonnaise to eggnog to Caesar dressing, are prepared with raw egg yolk, but technically only a fuly cooked egg is guaranteed to be free of salmonella. Consequently, raw or runny eggs are not recommended for infants, the elderly, pregnant women, or anyone with a weakened immune system.

10 BUY FRESH BREAD

Try to buy fresh loaves of interesting bread from an independent bakery or the bakery in your grocery store. Although fresh loaves don't last as long as sliced bread, they're much more enjoyable, and you can use the old stuff to make Panzanella (page 37), or Croutons or Breadcrumbs (page 158) to top other dishes. Later in the day, many independent bakeries offer deep discounts on bread they would otherwise have to throw out.

11 DON'T BUY DRINKS

All the body needs drink-wise is water. Except for milk, most packaged drinks are overpriced and deliver a lot of sugar without filling you up the way a piece of fruit or a bowl of yogurt would. If you want a special drink, make Agua Fresca (page 169), a smoothie (page 170), or tea.

12 GET CREATIVE WITH WILTED VEGETABLES

Sometimes you forget a pepper or bunch of spinach in the back of the fridge. Although wilted veggies might not remain fit for a salad, they'll still be wonderful in any dish that calls for sautéed, grated, or baked vegetables. Just cut off any actual rot. You can also use them in broth.

13 MAKE YOUR OWN BROTH

In almost any savory recipe that calls for water, homemade broth would be better. To make broth, start by saving any vegetable bits that you chop off and would normally throw away, like onion tops, the seedy parts of peppers, and the ends of carrots. Store them in the freezer until you have a few cups, then cover them with water, bring to a boil, and simmer over low heat for a few hours. Add salt to taste, and you have broth! To make a heartier broth, do the same with leftover bones or scraps of meat (preferably all the same kind of meat). Because you're using stuff you'd otherwise throw away, broth is effectively free.

14 TREAT YOUR FREEZER WITH RESPECT

A freezer can be a great friend for saving time by letting you prepare large batches of food at once. For instance, cooking dried beans takes a while (page 165), so make more than you need, then freeze the rest. Another great trick I learned from a reader is to dice a whole package of bacon, fry it, and then freeze it in small parcels. This makes it easy to add a small amount of bacon to a dish without the temptation of using the whole package or the fear of rancid meat.

15 TURN CHICKEN SKIN INTO SCHMALTZ

Schmaltz is rendered chicken fat that you can use like butter. Buy chicken that still has its skin, then trim the skins and lay them in a pan over low heat. Add a cup or so of water and simmer until the fat releases from the skin and the water cooks off. Let the fat cool, then throw away the skins and pour the fat into a glass jar. Store in the fridge.

16 BUY A PEPPER GRINDER

Seriously, banish pre-ground pepper from your life—it loses all flavor when it sits around. Fresh pepper creates pops of intensity on the tongue and lights up bland dishes. One of the most popular dishes in Rome is just pasta with butter and pepper: Give it a try!

17 BUY YOGURT IN BULK

There are so many types of yogurt in the grocery store: some low in fat and high in sugar, some with cute animal pictures. Some are Greek. Some have chocolate shavings and candy. Some have names like "Key lime pie." Now forget about all of that. The buckets of plain yogurt are the best value for your money. If you start with plain yogurt, you can make your favorite flavors in your own kitchen, where you know exactly what's going into it. The fat content is your choice.

If you have kids, ask them what flavors they can imagine and go make them! It's a lot more fun than letting the supermarket choose for you. Try something new and smash it in! If you want to make thicker Greek-style yogurt, all you have to do is strain the standard variety through cheesecloth to remove the extra water.

Yogurt's versatility makes it a great staple to keep in the fridge. And when you consider that there are savory options—like Tzatziki (page 146) or Raita (page 147)—the possibilities expand even more.

1. Bananas
2. Peanut butter
3. Frozen or dried fruit
4. Yogurt
5. Lime
6. Honey
7. Coconut
8. More yogurt!
9. Fresh berries
10. Kiwi fruit
11. Red and green grapes
12. Jam or jelly

SUPERMARKET STRATEGIES

With these commonly available items in your pantry, you can have a wide variety of meals on the table within minutes. Keeping a well-stocked pantry is the key to easy, fast cooking at home. When you're living on a budget, building up supplies does take time, but just keep adding each week and you'll get there.

1 PROTEIN

Meat isn't the only protein! Items like dried beans, nuts, and eggs are cheap, store easily, and have multiple uses. Be aware that most fish at the grocery store has previously been frozen and was merely thawed for display. There's no harm in buying it frozen and thawing it yourself.

2 DAIRY

Butter is just as good to cook with as it is on toast. The cheeses listed opposite are the ones I like best, but buy what your taste, budget, and local availability allow.

3 VEGETABLES

Vegetables can (and should!) be the base of most meals. Other than greens, which should be used quickly, they can be stored for a few days to a few weeks. Try to snag each vegetable as it hits peak season.

4 FRUITS

Citrus fruits are cooking essentials and they keep well. The zest and juice can liven up just about any dish, and they always make a great dressing. Bananas, apples, and melons are great quick snacks, but try every fruit you can afford! Remember, almost all fruits and vegetables have a season, so savor them at their freshest and cheapest.

5 GRAINS

Flour is so inexpensive, and once you have a few basics at hand, most baked goods are a cinch to make. There's great variety in whole grains. Substitute them for rice, toss them in a salad, or add them to soup.

6 CANNED VEGETABLES

Plenty of vegetables are good when canned, so remember to compare prices between fresh, frozen, and canned. The canned versions are fantastic in sauces. Just be aware that canned foods are often very salty, so you might want to rinse them, except for canned tomatoes.

7 FROZEN FRUITS AND VEGETABLES

Fresh berries can be expensive, but the frozen ones often go on sale and are great for smoothies. Frozen veggies are quick to add to soups and rice dishes. Compare prices to see whether frozen is the best value.

8 FLAVOR

You can explore an extraordinary number of cuisines with these items. They add depth and excitement to the simplest dishes.

9 TREATS THAT GO A LONG WAY

Although specialty items can be expensive, a little goes a long way. When you can, pick up an item or two and enjoy the results.

10 SPICES

Spices are expensive to buy and can often be a sticking point: no caloric value and they often have a high price tag. But because you use such small amounts, they end up costing pennies per recipe. If you're able to shop around, look for inexpensive spices in bulk at ethnic markets. I've suggested (opposite) the spices you should start with. I use these a lot in these recipes and at home. If you want to branch out further, take a look at page 149 to be inspired by flavor combinations.

GROCERIES YOU WON'T REGRET BUYING

PROTEIN
eggs
dried beans
lentils
tofu
nuts
peanut butter

DAIRY
butter
milk
yogurt
queso fresco
Romano or Parmesan cheese
sharp Cheddar cheese
mozzarella

VEGETABLES
garlic
onions
carrots
celery
peppers
broccoli
tomatoes
hot peppers
hardy greens
salad greens
potatoes
sweet potatoes
cauliflower
winter squash

FRUITS
apples
melons
oranges
limes
lemons
bananas

GRAINS
bread
tortillas
pasta
all-purpose flour
whole-wheat flour
oats
popcorn
short-grain rice
long-grain rice
brown rice
cornmeal
other dried whole grains

CANNED VEGETABLES
whole tomatoes
tomato paste
corn

**FROZEN FRUITS
AND VEGETABLES**
berries
peas
green beans
corn

FLAVOR
olive oil or vegetable oil
wine vinegar
anchovies
sardines
olives
fish sauce
coconut milk
miso paste
mustard
soy sauce
chili sauce
brown sugar
fresh herbs

**TREATS THAT GO
A LONG WAY**
dried fruits
dried mushrooms
frozen shrimp
maple syrup
bacon
vanilla extract
cocoa powder

SPICES
chile flakes
cinnamon
cumin or cumin seeds
paprika and smoked paprika
curry powder
oregano
thyme

LEFTOVERS

Leftovers may be convenient, but they can seem unappealing, limp, and cold after sitting in the fridge for a couple of days. That's why the sandwich, the wrap, and the taco are your friends. Here are just a few ideas for how to give leftovers a makeover very quickly to invent a whole new meal!

1 CHANA MASALA WRAP

Sounds strange, but trust me: Spread herbed mayo on the wrap and pile in the Chana Masala (page 109).

2 BLACK-EYED PEAS AND COLLARDS WRAP

Fold the Black-Eyed Peas and Collards (page 111) into a wrap with a little hot sauce or some Tzatziki.

3 TOMATO SCRAMBLED EGGS WRAP

Throw the Tomato Scrambled Eggs (page 2) into a wrap and add some roasted potatoes or rice for bulk.

4 VEGETABLE JAMBALAYA BURRITO

Add some salsa or any leftover beans to the Vegetable Jambalaya (page 99) and wrap in a flour tortilla.

5 CAULIFLOWER CHEESE SANDWICH

Start with Cauliflower Cheese (page 93), and add crunchy greens, toast, and mustard. Yum!

6 ROASTED VEGETABLE SANDWICH (PAGE 106)

Add some extra spices or sauces to liven up the vegetables and grill the bread for some crunch.

7 ROASTED POTATO AND CHILE TACO

This dish (page 65) is great in a taco: Just add a little salsa and grated cheese. I like green salsa here.

8 TILAPIA TACO

For a makeshift fish taco, add the Tilapia (page 85), Wilted Cabbage Salad (page 43), and cilantro to a tortilla and enjoy.

9 CAULIFLOWER TACOS

Combine Smoky and Spicy Roasted Cauliflower (page 51) with Salsa (page 145) and grated Cheddar or cotija cheese in a warm tortilla.

10 FANCIED-UP POUTINE

Pretend you're at a super-modern poutinery and make up some crazy toppings for your baked French fries. Black-Eyed Peas and Collards (page 111) would be great, as would Chili (page 131), Baked Beans (page 48), or Filipino Chicken Adobo (page 77).

11 JACKET SWEET POTATOES SPREAD

Mash up leftover baked Jacket Sweet Potatoes (page 64), then spread them in a bacon sandwich for a sweet counterpoint.

12 RETHINK TOAST TOPPINGS

Any of the recipes that can top Toast (page 68) would also be great over rice or any other grain, wrapped in a tortilla, tossed with pasta, or even on a pizza. Or, take a pack of ramen noodles, skip the flavor packet, and throw in one of the toast toppings instead.

13 CHILI THREE WAYS

Take some chili (page 131), stuff into Jacket Sweet Potatoes (page 64), serve over roasted vegetables, or top hot dogs.

14 REINVIGORATE VEGGIES

Got some veggies that look past their prime? Try them in any of the soups (pages 21–29) or Dark and Spicy Chili (page 131), Bubble and Squeak (page 63), in scrambled eggs (page 2), or cooked into a tomato sauce (page 127). The Broiled Eggplant Salad (page 32) is lovely tossed with noodles.

Mashed winter vegetables make a great pierogi filling (page 138), can be added to scrambled eggs (page 2), or used as a sandwich filling.

SEASONAL CHART

Here's a chart of some common fruits and vegetables with shading that represents the months when it's best to buy them. Generally, in-season produce is likely to be less expensive. Of course, where you live also makes a difference in cost, so make sure to check the specials when you go to the grocery store.

	JAN	FEB	MAR	APR	MAY	JUN	JUL	AUG	SEP	OCT	NOV	DEC
apple									X	X	X	
avocado			X	X	X	X	X	X	X	X		
beet									X	X		
bell peppers						X	X	X				
bok choy	X	X	X									
broccoli			X	X					X	X	X	
brussels sprouts	X	X									X	X
cabbage			X	X								
cauliflower												
collard greens	X	X	X									X
corn							X	X				
cucumber						X	X	X				
eggplant							X	X				
garlic						X	X	X				
green beans					X	X	X	X				
jalapeño peppers						X	X	X				
kale	X									X	X	X
leeks	X	X								X	X	X
lettuce												
mango				X	X							
mushroom	X											X
onion	X	X	X									
peaches						X	X	X				
peas				X	X	X						
potato	X											X
spinach			X	X						X	X	
summer squash						X	X	X	X			
sweet potatoes	X	X								X	X	X
tomato							X	X				
turnip	X	X								X	X	X
winter squash	X								X	X	X	X

KITCHEN EQUIPMENT

It might seem like a daunting task to stock your kitchen with equipment, but it doesn't need to be scary—or expensive. The tools below will help you make any recipe in this book.

❶ GOOD KNIVES

- A good chef's knife is the most important tool in your kitchen. Make sure it's big and sharp.
- You'll need a paring knife for smaller tasks, like peeling and coring an apple.
- Get a serrated knife to cut bread and tomatoes easily.

❷ BOX GRATER

Use it to:
- Grate cheese
- Shred potatoes
- Make quick work of tough vegetables

❸ MEASURING CUPS AND SPOONS

❹ ESSENTIAL POTS AND PANS

- Large cast-iron or nonstick pan
- Medium-size saucepan
- Large soup pot

❺ STIRRING UTENSILS

- You can stir anything with a long-handled wooden spoon.
- A ladle is essential for soups, stews, and sauces.
- While you can often use a fork instead, get a whisk if you're serious about sauces or desserts.

❻ ROASTING

- Use oven-safe dishes and baking pans—glass, ceramic, etc.—for broiling, baking, and roasting.
- Casserole dishes are handy for storing leftovers.

❼ SIEVE

Use it to:
- Drain pasta or boiled veggies
- Sift flour
- Strain extra whey from yogurt

❽ MICROPLANE

Use it to:
- Zest lemons and limes
- Grate hard cheeses and garlic
- Shred soft vegetables into a sauce

❾ SPECIALTY BAKING

- Muffin tins can be used for baking in small portions (not just muffins!).
- It's hard to make a cake without a cake pan.
- Rimmed baking sheets can also be used to roast veggies or broil fish.

❿ IMMERSION BLENDER

- Use it to puree soups and smoothies.
- It's more versatile and quicker to clean than traditional blenders.
- If you need power, consider investing in a food processor or full-size blender.

⓫ FLIPPING AND SHUFFLING UTENSILS

- Flat spatulas are for flipping pancakes.
- Rounded spatulas are good to scrape bowls.
- Use tongs for salads, or moving hot foods without hurting yourself.

⓬ CUTTING BOARD

- Wood is longest lasting and, contrary to what you might think, the most sanitary surface for preparing raw meat. There's a reason it's called butcher block!
- Cheap plastic boards are fine and easy to wash.
- Don't get glass. Just don't.

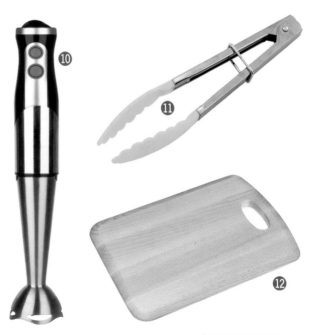

HOW TO USE THIS BOOK

Good and Cheap is a strategy guide, not a typical cookbook. Sure, we have *breakfast, dinner,* and *snacks and sides.* But there is also *big batch* for feeding a crowd or planning ahead. There is the *pantry* section filled with the staples we eat every day and the sauces that make those basics sing. The *drinks and desserts* are delicious and worth the effort, while making use of everyday ingredients you'll buy for other meals. The *ideas* pages show just how much variety there is in simple things like oatmeal or popcorn. And the *methods* are meant to teach you a process that you can use over and over again.

Once you embrace cooking, you learn that there are no rules for the best oatmeal, there's just *your* best oatmeal. More practically, you realize that many ingredients are used in similar ways and can be easily substituted. If there is a sale on red lentils or a neighbor gives you a bag of zucchini, I want you to be armed with the skills to take advantage of that, not shackled to an inflexible recipe. The recipes in this book are a starting point. My hope is that with *Good and Cheap* as a foundation, you'll learn to cook without recipes and be empowered to cook for your own pleasure.

BREAKFAST

Tomato Scrambled Eggs

This pile of fluffy, creamy eggs holds together a mass of tangy, juicy, sweet tomatoes. This dish is best enjoyed when tomatoes are in season. Serve the eggs on, in, or alongside some toast or a tortilla, if you have any on hand. SERVES 2

½ tablespoon butter

4 small or 2 large, chopped fresh tomatoes, or 2 cups chopped canned tomatoes

4 eggs

salt and pepper, to taste

ADDITIONS

sprinkling of chopped fresh basil or other herbs

1 Melt the butter in a small or medium nonstick pan over medium heat, swirling it around to coat the pan. Add the tomatoes and cook until they release their juice and most of it evaporates, 5 to 7 minutes.

2 Meanwhile, crack the eggs into a bowl and add a generous sprinkling of salt and pepper. Beat the eggs lightly with a fork.

3 Turn the heat down to low and add the eggs to the pan. Using a spatula, gently mix the eggs with the tomatoes and stir carefully and continuously, to keep the eggs from forming chunks. Turn the heat down as low as possible; the slower your eggs cook, the creamier they'll be.

4 Once the eggs are cooked to your desired consistency, turn off the heat and add any chopped herbs. Basil is the best with tomatoes. I like my scrambled eggs loose and juicy with the eggs forming very soft curds. You can let them cook a little longer if you prefer your eggs drier.

Omelet

I make this omelet at least once a week. It's insanely delicious, whether laden with veggies or kept simple. I love it with dill, but it's good with almost any herb, or with scallions. I tend to use Cheddar and Romano, since they go well with most vegetables. But other great combos are goat cheese with zucchini, and cauliflower with sausage and chile flakes.

If I'm serving two people, I usually cut one large omelet in half rather than making two. However, if you feel like being fancy, make a pair of two-egg omelets simply by using half the ingredients for each. For a French style omelet, roll it up in Step 4 instead of folding it. The result will be quite thin and tender. SERVES 2

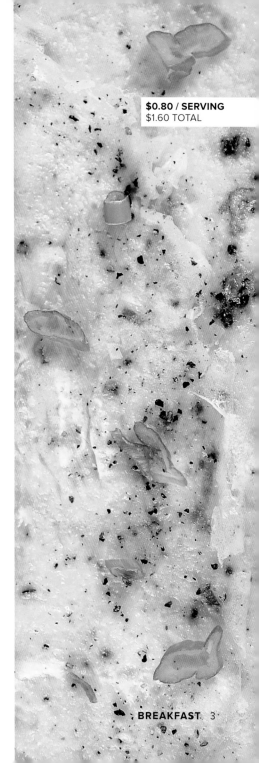

$0.80 / SERVING
$1.60 TOTAL

4 eggs

2 tablespoons finely chopped fresh dill

salt and pepper, to taste

butter, for the pan

1 shallot or ½ small red onion, finely diced

¼ cup grated cheese

1 Place the eggs, dill, salt, and pepper in a bowl, and beat with a fork.

2 Melt a small pat of butter in a big frying pan over medium-high heat. Once it's sizzling, add the shallot and sauté for about 2 minutes, until it's translucent and smells great.

3 Add the egg to the hot pan and swirl it to coat the surface evenly. If the center of the omelet cooks more quickly than the edge, use a spatula to pull any raw egg into the middle. Then stop touching it.

4 After about 30 seconds, toss the cheese on top of the egg, along with any other raw or cooked vegetable you feel like adding. Once none of the egg remains translucent, 30 seconds to 2 minutes, fold the omelet in half with your spatula and lift it out of the pan. You don't want any brown on your eggs.

Egg Sandwiches with Mushroom Hash

Egg sandwiches are a mainstay of every corner deli in New York City, and for good reason: They're cheap and easy, fast, and delicious. I knew I had to include one when Charlene, one of my early supporters, asked for a recipe with eggs and mushrooms. (I'm thankful she did! I don't really like mushrooms, so they're scarce in this book, even though plenty of people love them.) Like most sandwiches, this recipe is really flexible. In particular, you can change the hash to use whatever you have around. Sad leftovers take on new life when turned into a hash and matched with the rich fattiness of a runny egg. SERVES 2

2 teaspoons butter

1 small potato, diced

salt and pepper, to taste

8 ounces mushrooms, sliced

2 cloves garlic, finely chopped

2 rolls or English muffins, split, or 4 slices of bread

2 eggs

ADDITIONS

sliced tomato

pitted, peeled, and sliced avocado

cheese

VARIATIONS

potato and onion

potato and pea

collards and bacon

zucchini

chorizo and green chile

1 Melt 1 teaspoon of the butter in a pan over medium heat. Throw in the potato pieces and cook, stirring minimally, until they just start to brown and soften, about 5 minutes. Season them with salt and pepper.

2 Add the mushrooms and garlic and cook, stirring, until the mushrooms are brown and have shrunk down, another 5 minutes. If the potato pieces are getting stuck to the pan, add a splash of water. Pierce one piece of potato with a fork to test it. If it goes through easily, you're done. If not, cook for a few more minutes. (The smaller the potatoes are chopped, the quicker they'll cook.) Taste and adjust the seasoning to your preferences.

3 Place the rolls or bread in the toaster. Meanwhile, melt the other teaspoon of butter in a medium, nonstick skillet over medium heat. Crack the eggs in and dust with salt and pepper.

4 *If you like your eggs sunny-side up*, place a lid over the pan to ensure that the whites will cook through without making the yolks hard. Once the whites are no longer translucent, turn off the heat and remove the eggs from the pan.

If you like eggs over easy (my favorite), wait until the yolks are cooked but still look runny, then flip each egg with a spatula and let the other side cook for about 15 seconds. That'll get your whites fully cooked, but keep the yolks runny—the best. If you prefer hard yolks (please, no!), then cook for another 30 seconds.

5 Moving quickly so everything stays nice and hot, assemble the ingredients into a sandwich, layering the veggies first, topping with the egg, and using any condiments you like. Way better than what you'll find at the corner deli!

Peanut Butter and Jelly Granola Bars

Tired of endless PB+J sandwiches? Give these bars a try instead! I designed them for my friend Alex, the best long-distance runner I know. They are a little more crumbly than a store-bought granola bar, so be careful when eating these on the go—you'll probably leave a trail of crumbs on the sidewalk and down your shirt. As a bonus, you can find the ingredients in any corner store or food pantry. Any kind of jam or jelly will do—I used blueberry, but grape, strawberry, or any flavor would be tasty. You can use quick-cooking oats if they're all you have, but I prefer the bite and chew of rolled oats. For a little more crunch along with your chew, you can also substitute a cup of Rice Krispies for a cup of the oats. MAKES 12 BARS

butter or vegetable oil, for the pan

3 cups rolled oats, or 2 cups rolled oats and 1 cup Rice Krispies

½ cup peanut butter

½ cup jelly or jam

¼ cup hot water

¼ teaspoon salt

ADDITIONS

½ cup chopped nuts

½ cup shredded coconut

½ cup chopped dried fruit

½ cup honey (instead of the jelly)

1 Preheat the oven to 350°F.

2 Grease an 8- by 11-inch baking pan. If you have a different size pan, that's fine—it'll just change how thick the bars are, so you'll want to adjust the cooking time a little. A larger pan may take less time to cook through and get crunchy, while a smaller pan will take a few more minutes—just keep an eye on it in the oven.

3 Pour the oats into a large bowl.

4 Place a small saucepan over low heat and add the peanut butter, half of the jelly, the water, the salt, and any other additions. Stir until smooth, about 2 minutes.

5 Pour the peanut butter and jelly concoction into the oats and mix until all the oats are coated and you have a sticky mass. Dump the mixture into the buttered baking pan and press it into an even layer. Spread the remaining jelly over the top.

6 Pop the baking dish into the oven for 25 minutes. The bars are done when the edges are toasty and brown. Mmm. Crunchy.

7 Leave the bars in the pan until they cool completely, about an hour, then slice them into 12 bars.

$0.30 / BAR
$3.60 TOTAL

ideas
OATMEAL

Oatmeal is a hot and comforting breakfast that will give you energy for a great morning. It's also extremely inexpensive, so it will allow you to spend a bit more on lunch and dinner. Basic oatmeal has a reputation for being dull, but this recipe can be dressed up in so many ways, you'll never get bored.

Think of basic oatmeal as a foundation. Make it your own with the ideas on the next pages. Whether it's milky and sweet or savory and salty, I'm sure you can find a favorite way to enjoy a hot bowl of oats in the morning!

Basic Oatmeal

SERVES 2

1 cup rolled oats
2 cups water
¼ teaspoon salt

1 Add the oats, water, and salt to a small pot and bring to a boil over medium heat. Immediately turn the heat to low and place a lid on the pot.

2 Cook for 5 minutes, until the oats are soft and tender and most of the water has evaporated. You can add more water if you like your oatmeal smooth and thin, or use slightly less to make it thick and creamy.

❶ Pumpkin
$0.75 SERVING / $1.50 TOTAL

½ cup canned pumpkin
¾ cup milk (or almond milk or soy milk)
2 tablespoons brown sugar, plus more to taste
1 teaspoon ground cinnamon

ADDITIONS
¼ teaspoon ground ginger
¼ teaspoon ground cloves
drizzling of maple syrup

Whisk the pumpkin, milk, and 1¼ cups water (not the full 2 cups in the basic recipe) in a pot. Add the oats, salt, brown sugar, and spices. Cook over medium-low heat until the mixture just comes to a boil, 2 to 5 minutes. Turn to low for 5 more minutes. Add maple syrup or more sugar to taste.

❷ Savory
$0.75 SERVING / $1.50 TOTAL

2 or 3 scallions, white and green parts, finely chopped
¼ cup grated sharp Cheddar cheese
1 teaspoon butter
2 eggs

Cook the oatmeal as directed in basic oatmeal (left), adding the scallions in Step 1. Just before it's done, stir in the cheese. While the oatmeal cooks, melt the butter in a pan over medium heat. Crack in the eggs, then cover the pan and fry until the yolks are runny but the whites are cooked, 2 to 3 minutes. Top each bowl of oats with one fried egg!

❸ Coconut and Lime

$0.75 SERVING / $1.50 TOTAL

¼ cup unsweetened
   coconut flakes
2 tablespoons sugar
juice of ½ lime

Add the coconut and
sugar to the oatmeal, and
cook as directed in Basic
Oatmeal (page 9). Turn off
the heat and squeeze the
lime juice over the top.

❹ Fruity

$0.55 SERVING / $1.10 TOTAL

½ cup berries, or chopped
   fruit, fresh or frozen
1 tablespoon sugar

Cook the oatmeal as
directed in Basic Oatmeal
(page 9), but 2 minutes
before it's ready, add the
berries and sugar and stir
to combine. It's surprising
how many variations
you can come up with
just by trying a new fruit
or combining several
varieties.

❺ Apple Cinnamon

$1 SERVING / $2 TOTAL

2 cups apple juice or cider
1 teaspoon ground
   cinnamon
1 apple, cored and
   chopped

Cook the oats as directed
in Basic Oatmeal (page 9),
using the apple juice
instead of the water and
adding the cinnamon.
Top with the apple. If you
want the apple to be soft
and warm, cook it along
with the oats.

❻ Baklava

$0.75 SERVING / $1.50 TOTAL

1 teaspoon ground
   cinnamon
1 tablespoon finely grated
   orange zest
4 tablespoons honey
2 tablespoons chopped
   almonds or pistachios

Add the cinnamon, orange
zest, and 2 tablespoons of
the honey before cooking
the oatmeal as directed in
Basic Oatmeal (page 9).
Once it's done, top each
bowl with another
tablespoon of honey and
a tablespoon of nuts.

❼ Chocolate

$0.50 SERVING / $1 TOTAL

1 cup milk
1 tablespoon cocoa
1 tablespoon sugar

A brilliant suggestion from
a wonderful reader, Karen
Lofstrom. Who needs
Cocoa Puffs when you can
have cocoa oatmeal?

Replace one of the two
cups of water with 1 cup
of milk. Stir the cocoa and
sugar into the milk and
water before you add it
to the pan—this will keep
the lumps away! Then
proceed as usual with the
oatmeal (see page 9).

Breakfast Quinoa

Quinoa makes a great alternative to oatmeal from time to time. It contains more naturally occurring protein than oats do, so it keeps you full longer. Unfortunately, it also comes with a higher price tag, but if you buy in bulk, it can still be affordable. **SERVES 2**

1 cup white quinoa

2 cups water

¼ teaspoon salt

1 tablespoon sugar

1 cup berries or chopped fruit, fresh or frozen

1 Add the quinoa, water, and salt to a small pot and bring to a boil over medium heat. Turn the heat down to low. Place a lid on the pot, slightly askew, to let steam escape.

2 After about 10 minutes, add the sugar and half the fruit, stirring to combine. The quinoa should take about 20 minutes total, but keep an eye on it and add more water if it becomes too dry. It's ready when the grains are translucent, have doubled in size, and you can see an opaque ring around each grain.

3 Fluff up the quinoa with a fork and scoop it into bowls. Top with the rest of the fruit.

Banana Pancakes

With the creamy texture and delicious flavor of bananas, these pancakes are stunningly good. You will be seriously popular if you feed these to your family or friends. Another plus: This is a great way to get rid of mushy bananas that doesn't involve making banana bread. **SERVES 4, MAKES 10 TO 15 PANCAKES**

2 cups all-purpose flour

¼ cup brown sugar

2 teaspoons baking powder

1 teaspoon baking soda

1 teaspoon salt

4 bananas

2 eggs

1½ cups milk

1 teaspoon vanilla extract

butter, for cooking and serving

syrup, for serving

1 Preheat the oven on its lowest setting.

2 Combine the flour, brown sugar, baking powder, baking soda, and salt in a medium-size bowl. Mix thoroughly with a spoon.

3 In another medium bowl, mash 2 of the bananas with a fork. Add the eggs, milk, and vanilla, and mix well to combine.

4 Add the dry mixture to the bananas, stirring with a spoon until everything just comes together. Tender pancakes come from not overmixing the batter. If there are still a few pockets of flour, don't worry about it.

5 Let the mixture sit for 10 to 15 minutes. Meanwhile, slice the 2 remaining bananas.

6 Place a nonstick or cast-iron skillet or griddle over medium heat. Once it's hot, melt a small amount of butter, about ½ teaspoon, in the skillet and ladle some pancake batter into the center of the pan.

A normal amount of batter is ¼ to ⅓ cup, but you can make your pancakes as large or small as you like. If it's your first time making pancakes, make them smaller: They'll be easier to flip.

7 As soon as the batter is in the pan, place 3 to 4 banana slices atop the uncooked side of the pancake. Once the edges of the pancake start to dry up and you can see the middle start to bubble, flip the pancake over. Cook until it is browned on both sides, about 30 seconds to 1 minute per side.

8 Stack the finished pancake on a plate in the warm oven and repeat Steps 6 and 7 until you run out of batter. Serve hot, with butter and syrup.

IF YOU'RE IN A HURRY, use a larger skillet or griddle and cook a few pancakes at a time. Making batches of three or four is much faster than one pancake at a time!

Whole-Wheat Jalapeño Cheddar Scones

Spicy, cheesy, flaky—these scones are at their best straight out of the oven. They're delicious for breakfast, or with a plate of beans or a pile of vegetables, or crumbled into stew or chili (page 131). Cutting the cheese into cubes rather than grating it means you'll have pockets of gooey cheese that contrast nicely with the crumb of the scone. If you want the heat of the jalapeño, leave the seeds and membrane; if you like it milder, remove them and chop up only the pepper itself. **MAKES 6 SCONES**

½ cup (1 stick) butter (see box)

2½ cups whole-wheat flour,
   plus more for the work surface

1 tablespoon baking powder

1 teaspoon salt

1 jalapeño pepper, finely chopped
   (see headnote)

4 ounces sharp Cheddar cheese,
   diced to about ¼ inch

2 eggs, lightly beaten

½ cup milk

EGG WASH (OPTIONAL)

1 egg

salt and pepper, to taste

USE THE WRAPPER from the
stick of butter to grease the baking
sheet.

---

1 Place the butter in the freezer for 30 minutes.

2 Preheat the oven to 400°F. Line a baking sheet with parchment paper or lightly grease it with butter.

3 Combine the flour, baking powder, and salt in a large bowl.

4 Remove the butter from the freezer and grate it directly into the flour mixture. (Use a cheese grater—it's the best way to break up butter without melting it.) Using your hands, gently squish the butter into the flour until everything is incorporated but not smooth. The chunks of butter will create flaky scones.

5 Add the jalapeño, cheese, beaten eggs, and milk to the bowl, then use your hands to mix everything gently until it just comes together. The dough will probably be a little shaggy, but that's fine.

6 Sprinkle flour on a clean countertop and dump the dough onto it. Gently shape the dough into a disk about 1½ inches thick. Cut the disk into 6 triangular wedges, like a pizza, and move them to the baking sheet.

7 If you want to make the egg wash (recommended!), lightly beat the egg and brush it over the scones (you'll have more egg wash than you need to use). Sprinkle salt and pepper over each scone. Bake for 25 minutes or until golden brown.

Chocolate Zucchini Muffins

When my friend Michael challenged me to create a recipe that used dark chocolate, I got a little worried: Dark chocolate is expensive! But then I remembered that cocoa powder is deeply, darkly chocolaty, without the expense. I thought of the chocolate zucchini cake my mother made when I was growing up and knew I had something.

This is a great breakfast treat that uses staples you should generally have on hand, such as flour, oats, and yogurt. The yogurt and zucchini make these muffins super moist and yummy, but still a reasonably nutritious (if slightly sugary) choice for breakfast. Make them in midsummer, during the height of zucchini season, when larger zucchini are really cheap. Big zucchini are generally a bit woodier, but they're great for baking.

MAKES 24 SMALL MUFFINS

---

butter or vegetable oil,
    for the muffin tin
2 cups grated zucchini
    (start with 1 large or
    2 small zucchinis)
1½ cups all-purpose flour
1½ cups rolled oats
1½ cups sugar
½ cup cocoa powder
2 teaspoons baking soda
1 teaspoon salt
4 eggs
1 cup plain yogurt

ADDITIONS
1 tablespoon ground cinnamon
½ cup dark chocolate chips

1 Preheat the oven to 350°F.

2 Grease 24 muffin cups with butter, or, if you have paper liners on hand, line the muffin cups.

3 Cut off the round end of the zucchini (which is a little tough), keeping the stem to use as a handhold. Shred the zucchini with a box grater into a large bowl, stopping before you get to the stem.

4 Dump the flour, oats, sugar, cocoa powder, baking soda, salt, and cinnamon and chocolate chips, if using, into a medium bowl.

5 Mix the eggs and yogurt with the grated zucchini. Add the dry ingredients, mixing until just combined.

6 With a spoon, dollop the batter into the muffin tins until each cup is about three-quarters full. Transfer to the oven and bake for 20 minutes.

7 Pull the muffins out and poke them in the middle with a toothpick or knife. If it comes out wet, bake the muffins for 5 more minutes. If it comes out clean, they're done.

8 Let the muffins cool in their tins for 20 to 30 minutes, then eat warm!

Broiled Grapefruit

If your oven has a broiler, this is a fast and fun way to liven up a standard, healthy breakfast of grapefruit, turning it into a hot and sticky treat. It might just make a grapefruit lover out of you! If you have maple syrup on hand, use it instead of sugar for even more flavor. SERVES 2

2 grapefruits
2 tablespoons light or dark brown sugar
salt

1 Turn your oven's broiler up to high.

2 Cut each grapefruit in half at the equator and place the halves, cut sides up, on a rimmed baking sheet or another ovenproof pan. Sprinkle the halves evenly with brown sugar and top with just a tiny bit of salt to bring out the flavor.

3 Place the grapefruit halves under the broiler until they turn bubbly and a little brown (or even black) around the edges. This usually takes me about 3 minutes, but every broiler is different, so monitor it— yours may take up to 8 minutes. Don't get distracted! Black on the edges is okay; black sticky mess in the center is not. Overbroiling ruins a good meal fast.

4 Let the grapefruit cool down for a minute or two before serving.

SOUP
AND SALAD

Dal

This thick lentil soup is a flavor-packed staple of the Indian table. There are a ton of ways to prepare dal, but the core—beyond the lentils themselves—is usually fresh ginger, garlic, and chile, along with some dry spices. You can use any type of lentil you like. If you're using larger lentils (like chana dal, French lentils, or split mung beans), soak them for 30 minutes. If you're using the small orange lentils, then don't bother soaking them—they cook very quickly. SERVES 4

1 tablespoon butter

1 medium onion, finely chopped

1 teaspoon cumin seeds

1 teaspoon black mustard seeds

1 teaspoon turmeric

2 cloves garlic, finely chopped

1 jalapeño or serrano pepper,
   finely chopped (see box)

½-inch piece of ginger, grated

2 cups lentils

salt and pepper, to taste

ADDITIONS

heavy cream

sprinkling of chopped fresh cilantro

sprinkling of chopped scallions

1 Melt the butter in a medium-size pot over medium heat. Add the onion and cook for 1 minute, then add the cumin seeds and mustard seeds and stir them until they sizzle. Toss in the turmeric, garlic, and jalapeño and cook until the vegetables soften, 3 to 4 more minutes. Add the ginger and stir-fry for about 30 seconds.

2 Add the lentils along with enough water to cover them, then cook, covered, until the lentils are tender, about 20 minutes for split red lentils, 30 for green or brown, or 45 for other whole varieties. Plan according to what lentil you are using (package directions can be helpful).

3 Sample the dal and add salt and pepper to taste. You'll probably need a fair bit of salt to bring out all the flavors—a teaspoon or so.

4 Top the dish with a splash of cream, some chopped fresh cilantro or scallions, and serve.

IF YOU PREFER MILD DISHES, use a quarter of the jalapeño to start and add more if you decide you like it. Serrano peppers are hotter than jalapeños, so only use those if you like your food very spicy. Like salt, the amount of chile pepper should be to your taste. And you can always seed and devein your peppers to reduce their heat.

Corn Soup

This thick, sweet, satisfying soup is a favorite of kids and adults. It's wonderful to make in late summer to early autumn when corn on the cob is at its peak, but canned or frozen corn can also serve as a warm reminder of summer in the depths of winter. If you're making this soup with corn on the cob, the first step is to make corn broth out of the cobs once you've removed the kernels. If you're using canned or frozen corn, you'll need to substitute chicken or vegetable broth instead. Pair it with a slice of garlic bread or add a hard-boiled egg for extra protein. SERVES 4 TO 6

1 tablespoon butter

1 onion, finely chopped

2 stalks of celery, finely chopped

1 green or red bell pepper, stemmed, seeded, and finely chopped

1 small potato, diced

4 cloves garlic, finely chopped

1 chile pepper, finely chopped (optional)

4 cups corn, fresh (from 4 to 8 ears), canned, or frozen

1 tablespoon cornmeal or all-purpose flour

5 cups corn broth (recipe follows), vegetable broth, or chicken broth

salt and pepper, to taste

1 Melt the butter in a large pot with a lid over medium heat. Add the onion, celery, bell pepper, and potato and stir. Cover the pot and let everything cook until the onion is translucent, about 5 minutes.

2 Remove the lid and add the garlic and the chile pepper, if using. Stir the vegetables, adding a splash of water or broth to free any that get stuck to the bottom of the pot.

3 Let the vegetables cook, stirring occasionally, until they are lightly browned and soft, 5 minutes more. The potatoes should not yet be fully cooked.

4 Add the corn and cornmeal to the pot and stir. Pour in the broth and bring to a boil, then turn the heat down to low and simmer until the broth thickens and becomes opaque, about 30 minutes.

5 Add salt and pepper. If you made your own corn broth, you'll probably need at least a teaspoon of salt; if you used store-bought broth, you'll need less.

Corn Cob Broth

MAKES 5 CUPS

4 to 8 corn cobs, kernels reserved for the soup (see box, page 40)

2 bay leaves (optional)

salt and pepper, to taste

Place the corn cobs and the bay leaves, if using, in a large stockpot and cover with water. Bring to a boil over high heat, then turn the heat down to medium and let boil for about 30 minutes. Taste the broth and add salt and pepper until it has a nice corn flavor. Measure out 5 cups of broth for the soup and store the rest. If you don't want to have leftovers, boil the broth longer, until it is reduced to 5 cups. This will make the flavor of the broth stronger. The broth will keep for several months in the freezer, or for a few weeks in the refrigerator.

$1.50 / **SERVING**
$9 TOTAL

French Onion Soup

Best if you accept it now: You are going to cry making this recipe, because the first step is to chop a mountain of onions. But crying is good for us from time to time. Soon you will be on to the magical part, watching a colossal pile of onions shrink and caramelize to make a sweet, flavorful, wonderful soup. Save this recipe for the winter, when other vegetables are out of season and you want to fill your home with rich aromas. As my friend Marilyn, who suggested this recipe, says, "The smell in your kitchen is absolute heaven." SERVES 6

4 pounds onions, any type

4 cloves garlic

2 tablespoons butter

2 bay leaves

3 teaspoons salt, plus more to taste

2 teaspoons pepper, plus more to taste

6 slices bread

1½ cups grated Gruyère or Cheddar cheese

ADDITIONS

beef broth or chicken broth instead of water in Step 4

½ cup red wine, or 1 tablespoon vinegar, any type

1 teaspoon chile flakes

sprinkling of fresh thyme leaves

1 Chop each onion in half from tip to tail, peel them, then slice them into approximately ¼-inch-thick (or smaller) half-moon slices. Big slices are fine since you're cooking the onions for so long. Slice the garlic as well.

2 Melt the butter in a large pot over medium heat. Add the onions, garlic, and bay leaves. Cover the pot with a lid and leave it until the onions release a lot of moisture, about 10 minutes. Give them a stir.

3 Cook for 1 to 1½ hours, stirring every 20 minutes. When the onions at the bottom start to stick and turn dark, add a splash of water to unstick them. Don't worry, they aren't burning, just caramelizing. The water helps lift off the sticky, delicious, sweet part!

4 Once the onions are very dark and about a quarter the volume they once were, add 8 cups of water, the salt, and the pepper. Bring to a boil and cover the pot again, turn the heat down to low, and let it simmer for another hour.

5 Taste and adjust with salt and pepper as needed, then ladle the soup into bowls. Discard the bay leaves.

6 Now it's time to make cheese toast! If you want classic French onion soup—with the toast directly in the soup, which makes it a bit soggy—place a piece of bread on top of each (ovenproof!) bowl of soup, sprinkle with cheese, then heat the bowls under the broiler until the cheese is bubbly, 2 to 5 minutes. If you don't like soggy toast, just broil the cheese toast on its own and serve it on the side to dunk.

> **IF YOU'RE USING ANY OF THE ADDITIONS,** add them with the water (or broth) in Step 4. The beef broth is traditional and will make the soup richer. The vinegar adds a nice hit of acidity, which provides some depth. The chile flakes or thyme add another dimension to the soup.

Lightly Curried Butternut Squash Soup

Squash is a wonderful vegetable for soup: It's flavorful and has a divinely smooth texture when cooked and pureed. Serve this soup to people who think they don't like squash or curry, and you'll change some minds. You can substitute any winter squash for the butternut—I just like butternut because it's faster to peel and chop than its many cousins. SERVES 4

1 butternut squash or equivalent amount of other winter squash (about 2 pounds)

1 tablespoon butter

1 medium onion, chopped

1 green bell pepper, stemmed, seeded, and chopped

3 cloves garlic, finely chopped

1 teaspoon ground cumin

1 teaspoon ground coriander

1 teaspoon ground turmeric

1 teaspoon cayenne pepper

1 can coconut milk, 2 tablespoons reserved for garnish

salt and pepper, to taste

ADDITIONS

sour cream

chopped scallions

chopped fresh cilantro

1 To prepare the squash, peel off the tough skin with a potato peeler. Cut the squash in half lengthwise with a sharp chef's knife, then scoop out the seeds and goop. (You can save the seeds for a tasty snack later, if you like—see page 52.)

2 Next, slice off the stem and the very bottom of the squash and throw them away. Place each half of the squash flat side down on a cutting board. Chop each half into ½-inch slices, then cut each slice into cubes.

3 Melt the butter in a large pot over medium heat. Add the onion, bell pepper, and garlic and sauté until translucent, about 2 minutes.

4 Add the cubed squash, cumin, coriander, turmeric, and cayenne, and stir it all together. Put a lid on the pot and cook for 2 minutes more. Add the coconut milk and 3 cups of water and stir.

5 Bring the soup to a boil, then turn down the heat to low and let it cook until the squash is tender, about 30 minutes. Taste the soup and add salt and pepper as needed. Soup usually needs a fair bit of salt to bring out the flavors, so be generous.

6 If you have an immersion blender, you can puree the soup in the pot. If you have a stand blender, wait until the soup has cooled before transferring it to the blender. Puree until smooth, then taste again and add any more salt and pepper if needed. You can enjoy the soup as is or serve it with a drizzle of the reserved coconut milk or a dollop of sour cream, plus some chopped scallions or cilantro.

$1.50 / SERVING
$6 TOTAL

Tomato Soup and Grilled Cheese

If I get to choose, this will be my last meal on earth. Some of the first "cooking" I did for myself, at age ten or so, was plopping out a can of tomato soup. I felt very adult. Now that I know how easy it is to make from scratch, I never bother with the canned stuff. And if your family is anything like mine, making a grilled cheese sandwich will get you more glory and appreciation than a four-course dinner you slaved over for hours. To me, everything that is good and honest, delicious and comforting, is contained in velvety tomato soup and a crusty grilled cheese sandwich.

The sandwich recipe makes five sandwiches, so adjust according to your needs. Use any good melting cheese, or a blend of cheeses. If you have just the ends of a few cheeses left over from other meals, this is a great way to use them. For the bread, I like rye, but anything will do. SERVES 5

The Soup

1 tablespoon butter

2 medium onions, chopped

4 cloves garlic, finely chopped

2 cans (28 ounces each) pureed tomatoes (see box)

6 cups vegetable broth (homemade is great, but a bouillon cube dissolved in water works just fine)

salt and pepper, to taste

ADDITIONS

½ cup heavy cream, to make cream of tomato soup

leaves from 2 sprigs fresh thyme

2 tablespoons chopped fresh basil

zest of 1 lemon

1 Melt the butter in a large pot over medium heat. Add the onions, stir them to coat, then place a lid on the pot and leave it for 5 minutes. Take the lid off and stir the onions. Add the garlic and cover again until the onions are soft and just starting to brown, another 2 minutes.

2 Add the pureed tomatoes and vegetable broth to the pot and stir, being sure to scrape any sticky onions off the bottom to keep them from burning. Bring the soup to a boil, then turn it down to low to simmer for about 10 minutes.

3 Taste and add salt and pepper as needed. Add the cream, herbs, or lemon zest, if using. For smooth soup, use an immersion blender to quickly puree the onions into the tomato mixture. If you're using a standard blender, wait for the soup to cool before you blend it.

> **I PREFER** to puree canned whole tomatoes in a blender or food processor—the quality is better than the ones already pureed in the can.

The Sandwiches

softened butter, for the bread

10 slices bread

Dijon mustard (optional)

2½ cups grated cheese (see headnote)

1 Spread the butter on one side of each slice of bread, all the way to the edges.

2 Flip over 5 slices, buttered side down, and top each with mustard, if using, and then with approximately ½ cup of the cheese. Top each of your cheesified slices with another piece of bread, buttered side up.

3 Place a pan over medium heat for about a minute (see box). Stuff as many sandwiches into the pan as you can fit. I usually don't do more than 3 at a time so there's room to flip them.

4 Fry the sandwiches until they turn golden brown, about 2 minutes. Press down gently on the top of each sandwich for even browning. Flip the sandwiches over with a spatula and repeat on the other side. Press down again to make sure that the cheese in the middle is melting. If either side is not as golden brown as you would like, flip that side down and cook it some more.

5 Once the sandwich is golden and the cheese is melted in the middle, serve it up with the soup. Dunking is optional.

> **IF YOUR PAN IS TOO HOT ON THE BOTTOM,** it will burn the sandwich before the cheese melts, so start with medium heat and lower the temperature as necessary. Placing a lid over your pan will trap some steam and melt the cheese faster.

Sweet or Savory Pineapple Salad

Pineapple is so sweet, juicy, and crunchy that its citric acid punch can sneak up on you—suddenly, you realize you can't feel your lips or the tip of your tongue anymore! Canned pineapple is rarely as strongly flavored and acidic as its fresh cousin, but it sure is convenient and affordable—plus, you get juice. Here are two quick and simple ways to add flavor to a good old can of pineapple. The sweet version makes a great dessert, snack, or even a topping for yogurt. The savory version is lovely on its own, almost like a pineapple salsa. Enjoy it on seafood or pork, or with beans in a taco. SERVES 2 AS A SIDE

Sweet

1 can pineapple, in juice
1 tablespoon sugar
zest of ½ lime
salt, a wee pinch

Savory

1 can pineapple, in juice
1 tablespoon finely chopped
  red chile
2 tablespoons chopped fresh
  cilantro
salt, to taste

1 Open the can of pineapple. Drain the juice into a glass and drink it!

2 If the pineapple is cut into chunks, simply scoop them into a bowl. If you have rings, chop them into bite-size pieces first.

3 Add the remaining ingredients for the sweet or savory salad. Stir and taste. For the sweet, don't forget the salt—it brings out the sweetness in the acidic pineapple. Adjust to taste, and serve.

Kale Caesar Salad

This kale is treated like romaine lettuce in a classic Caesar salad, not the creamy modern version. The bitterness of the greens is delicious alongside the rich, fatty dressing. You could also use Swiss chard. If you're worried about the raw egg yolk in the dressing, simply omit it. And make the croutons first—they'll take longest.

SERVES 2, OR 4 AS A SIDE

1 raw egg yolk, from a high-quality fresh egg

2 teaspoons lemon juice

2 teaspoons Dijon mustard

3 tablespoons olive oil

salt and pepper, to taste

1 large bunch kale

Croutons (page 158), about 2 cups

freshly grated Romano cheese

ADDITIONS

1 clove garlic, grated

1 anchovy fillet, chopped

1 Drop the egg yolk into a large mixing bowl. Add the lemon juice, mustard, and garlic and anchovy, if using. Whisk briskly until the dressing is light and frothy. Slowly add the olive oil, whisking the whole time. Once everything is incorporated, add the salt and pepper, then adjust to your taste. I like it very lemony.

2 Remove the large stem from the center of the kale leaves. (Lacinato kale, sometimes called Tuscan or dinosaur kale, has the easiest stems to remove.) Chop the leaves in half lengthwise, then cut into thin ribbons. This method disguises the kale's tough texture.

3 Toss the kale in the bowl to coat it with dressing. Set it aside for 10 minutes or leave it in the fridge for up to 4 hours. The kale will become tender as it marinates.

4 Before serving, toss in the croutons and a sprinkling (or more!) of Romano cheese, according to your taste.

Broiled Eggplant Salad

Eggplant haters often cite mushy texture as their biggest complaint. Well, this salad has you covered. Broiled eggplant has a crunchy and meaty texture, and the tahini dressing makes the salad rich and creamy. To turn it from a side into a lunchtime salad, throw in some roasted potatoes or chickpeas. SERVES 2 AS A SIDE

1 medium eggplant, sliced into circles
1 tablespoon tahini
1 tablespoon lemon juice
salt and pepper, to taste
chopped scallions

ADDITIONS
sprinkling of chile flakes
finely chopped fresh dill
roasted potatoes
chickpeas

1 Turn your oven's broiler to high. Arrange the slices of eggplant on a baking sheet, then place them under the broiler for 3 to 8 minutes, depending on the power of your broiler. (If you want the eggplant to get some char, position it as close to the broiler as possible.) Watch carefully. Once the eggplant begins to blacken, remove it from the oven and flip the slices over.

2 Repeat the process on the other side. Once your eggplant is nicely charred, chop it into bite-size pieces.

3 In a medium-size bowl, mix the tahini, lemon juice, and chile flakes, if using, and toss in plenty of salt and pepper. Add the eggplant and stir. Add more salt or lemon juice according to your taste. Top it with scallions, or dill, if available, and serve!

Beet and Chickpea Salad

This dish is spicy, crunchy, and almost certainly the pinkest salad you'll ever eat! Don't be scared. **SERVES 2 AS A SIDE**

$1.75 / SERVING
$3.50 TOTAL

2 or 3 beets
1 cup chickpeas, cooked
   or canned, drained
3 tablespoons peanuts

DRESSING
1 tablespoon fresh lime juice
1 teaspoon chili sauce
1 tablespoon olive oil
salt and pepper, to taste

1 Peel the raw beets, removing the stems if necessary, then shred them with a box grater. Place the shredded beets in a medium-size bowl along with the chickpeas and peanuts.

2 Stir the lime juice, chili sauce, olive oil, and salt and pepper together in a small bowl to make the dressing. Taste and adjust the salt and pepper to your liking.

3 Add the dressing to the bowl with the beets and mix to combine. Let everything sit about 5 minutes so that the flavors can soak into the vegetables and the beet juices can mingle with the dressing.

Ever-Popular Potato Salad

I developed this recipe because I'm not a big fan of mayonnaise-based potato salads. It's really the simplest thing: just potatoes in a regular vinaigrette. Smaller potatoes are best, but whatever you have will be fine! You can add all kinds of extras to make it more festive, but people always rave about the salad as is. The secret is that potatoes actually have really nice flavor—all you have to do is season them properly. Let potatoes be potatoes, no need to disguise 'em!

If you have leftover roasted potatoes or other root vegetables, the same idea works well. Just skip the cooking part and go straight to the dressing. SERVES 4 AS A SIDE

2 pounds potatoes

2 tablespoons olive oil

2 tablespoons lemon juice, lime juice, or vinegar

2 teaspoons Dijon mustard

salt and pepper, to taste

3 or 4 scallions

ADDITIONS

chopped fresh dill

chopped fresh parsley

paprika

finely chopped fresh chiles

finely chopped pickles

1 If you're using very large potatoes, chop them into halves or quarters to speed up the cooking—or dice them into bite-size pieces if you're really in a hurry. Otherwise, keep the potatoes whole.

2 Put the potatoes in a large pot with a lid and cover with water. Bring to a boil over medium-high heat, then turn the heat down to medium and set the lid askew so that steam can escape.

3 After boiling about 25 minutes, stab the largest potato with a fork. If the fork pierces the potato easily, it's fully cooked. If not, boil for 5 more minutes. It's fine if they're a little overcooked, but undercooked potatoes are awful.

4 Drain the potatoes. Once they're cool enough to handle safely (but still warm), roughly chop them into bite-size pieces (unless you did that in Step 1).

5 While the potatoes are cooling, mix the olive oil, lemon juice, mustard, salt, and pepper in a large bowl. Whisk it briskly until the liquid is blended. If you don't have a whisk, use a fork.

6 Throw the potatoes into the bowl and toss them in the dressing to coat. Add a generous amount of salt as you stir. Potatoes are very bland without salt! Let them marinate for 10 minutes.

7 Meanwhile, remove the outer layer and any wilty top bits from the scallions, chop them, and sprinkle them over the top. Toss the salad once more (along with any additions you are using), then taste and adjust the salt, pepper, and citrus juice or vinegar as you see fit. This keeps very well, covered, in the fridge for up to a week, and it travels nicely to a picnic or potluck. Have fun!

Spicy Panzanella

A former classmate of mine, George, likes salads with a little kick. (As you can maybe tell, I do, too!) For inspiration, I turned to panzanella, a classic Italian bread-and-tomato salad. The Italians are true masters of making leftovers delicious. Here, old hard bread soaks up tomato juice and dressing for a super-flavorful and filling salad. You can toss in any vegetable or fruit as long as it's juicy. Bell peppers or carrots won't work so well, but peaches, grapes, and zucchini all do. If you don't like spicy salads as much as George and I do, feel free to seed and stem the jalapeño to remove its fierce heat, or replace it entirely with garlic or shallot. SERVES 4 AS A SIDE

2 small field cucumbers or 1 English cucumber

2 medium tomatoes, chopped

salt and pepper, to taste

4 slices day-old bread

DRESSING

2 tablespoons olive oil, plus a few drops for the pan

1 jalapeño, finely chopped

2 tablespoons chopped tomato

salt and pepper, to taste

juice of 1 lime

ADDITIONS

chopped fresh herbs

chopped peaches, nectarines, or plums

finely chopped red onion

chopped zucchini or summer squash

pitted olives

grapes

1 If you're using field cucumbers—usually cheaper than English—peel them to remove the tough skin. (A little leftover peel is not a problem.) For English cucumbers, there's no need to peel.

2 Reserve about 2 tablespoons of the chopped tomatoes to use in the dressing, but throw the rest of the tomatoes and all of the cucumbers into a large bowl. Sprinkle generously with salt and pepper; the salt helps draw out the juices. Toss the vegetables and set aside.

3 Place a small saucepan over medium heat and add a few drops of olive oil. Add the jalapeño and sauté until it sizzles and smells good, about a minute, then add the rest of the chopped tomato and a tablespoon of water. Cook until the tomato juices release, another 2 minutes. Sprinkle liberally with salt and pepper.

4 Once the water has evaporated, turn off the heat and dump the jalapeño-tomato mixture on your cutting board. Chop it up very finely, then throw it back into the pan—with the heat off—with the lime juice and 2 tablespoons of olive oil. Stir to combine, taste, and add salt and pepper as needed. You've got dressing!

5 Chop or tear the bread into bite-size pieces, then toast it in a skillet over medium heat, tossing occasionally, until the bread chunks are toasty on all sides. Alternatively, just toast full slices of bread in a toaster and tear them up afterward, or skip the toasting if the bread is already super-hard.

6 Add the bread and dressing to the vegetables and stir to combine. Taste and adjust the salt and pepper once more. Let the salad sit for a few minutes so that the bread can soak up the juices, then serve!

$2.50 / SERVING
$5 TOTAL

Cold (and Spicy?) Asian Noodles

No question—cold but spicy food is refreshing and delicious on a hot summer day. Here's a recipe that you can really make your own. Use whatever sauce or dressing you like and whatever vegetables you have around, or just a few scallions. If you have some Spice Oil (page 151) on hand, be sure to add it. It's amazing in this.

SERVES 2, OR 4 AS A SIDE

12 ounces dried spaghetti, soba, or any Asian noodles

2 tablespoons soy sauce

1 bunch scallions, chopped

1 cucumber, finely chopped

salt and pepper, to taste

ADDITIONS

Spice Oil (page 151)

Peanut Sauce (page 143)

grated carrot

chopped hard-boiled egg

1 Prepare the noodles according to the package instructions. Rinse them under cold water and drain in a colander.

2 Put the noodles in a bowl and add the soy sauce, Spice Oil if you have it, scallions, and cucumber (and any other additions), and mix with a fork or tongs. Taste it and add salt and pepper or more Spice Oil as needed.

3 Let the noodles sit in the fridge for about an hour if you can. The flavors will mingle and become more intense. The finished dish should keep for up to 3 days, covered, in the fridge. A great make-ahead lunch.

Taco Salad

This salad is a great use for leftover beans or pulled pork—crunchy, fresh, yet satisfying enough to be a whole meal. I like to make taco salad for a weekday lunch in the summertime. SERVES 2, OR 4 AS A SIDE

4 cups chopped lettuce

1 cup cooked beans, pulled pork, or ground beef

2 small tomatoes, chopped

½ cup corn kernels, canned or fresh

2 or 3 scallions, finely chopped

1 cup tortilla chips, roughly crushed

¼ cup shredded sharp Cheddar cheese or queso fresco

DRESSING

¼ cup sour cream or yogurt

juice of 1 lime

salt and pepper, to taste

ADDITIONS

chopped cucumber

chopped jalapeño (remove seeds for less heat)

bell peppers, stemmed, seeded, and chopped

grated carrots

Salsa (page 145)

1 Mix the lettuce, beans, tomatoes, corn, scallions, tortilla chips, cheese, and any additions in a large bowl.

2 In a small bowl, stir together the sour cream, lime juice, salt, and pepper. Taste it and adjust the salt, pepper, and lime to your liking.

3 Just before serving, pour the dressing over the salad and toss to coat. Eat immediately, maybe with a few extra chips on the side.

Charred Summer Salad

One of the early supporters of this book, Gina, can't eat gluten and wanted more Mexican-inspired options. I designed this spicy summer salad for her, topped with popcorn for the kind of crunch that croutons would provide. Use smaller zucchini, and save the big ones for Chocolate Zucchini Muffins (page 16). If you own a grill, use it instead of the broiler! **SERVES 2, OR 4 AS A SIDE**

---

3 small or 2 medium zucchini

2 ears corn

1 tablespoon olive oil
  or vegetable oil

salt and pepper, to taste

2 ounces crumbled cotija or
  feta cheese

1 cup popped Popcorn (page 54)

DRESSING

juice of 1 lime

1 tablespoon olive oil

½ teaspoon chili powder,
  plus more for dusting

salt and pepper, to taste

1 Turn your oven's broiler to high.

2 Chop off both ends of the zucchini, then slice each into four long sticks. Shuck the corn. Lay the zucchini and corn on a baking sheet, then rub them with the oil, making sure they're well coated. Sprinkle with salt and pepper.

3 Broil the zucchini and corn for 2 to 5 minutes, depending on how powerful your broiler is. The zucchini should start to blacken in some spots. This is good! Turn the corn over as needed (but not the zucchini!) to make sure it cooks evenly. Broil until the vegetables are lightly charred, another 2 to 5 minutes. Let them cool.

4 To make the dressing, mix the lime juice, olive oil, chili powder, salt, and pepper in a large bowl. Taste it and adjust the seasoning, if necessary.

5 Chop the zucchini into bite-size pieces and slice the corn kernels from the cobs (see box).

6 Transfer the vegetables into the bowl with the dressing. Add the crumbled cotija or feta and mix well. Sprinkle the popcorn over the top, then dust with a little extra chili powder, salt, and pepper.

TO CUT THE KERNELS OFF A COB OF CORN, hold the cob by the stem, vertically, inside a large bowl. Rest the other end of the corn on the bottom of the bowl. Using a sharp knife, slice the kernels off the cob as far down as you can go until your wrist hits the lip of the bowl. Slice all the way around the cob. Flip the cob over vertically and slice off the kernels that you missed closer to the pointy end.

$1.05 / SERVING
$4.20 TOTAL

Wilted Cabbage Salad

The idea for this recipe came from a wonderful reader, Karen. Wilted cabbage keeps its crunch and freshness for several days, whereas a regular lettuce salad turns gross soon after being dressed. (Kale behaves similarly to cabbage—it's one of the reasons I love the kale salad on page 31!) This salad is best if left to marinate in the tart dressing overnight. Just be sure to add the peanuts shortly before serving to prevent sogginess.

SERVES 4 AS A SIDE

1 medium-size cabbage,
  finely chopped
1 tablespoon salt
½ cup raw peanuts
½ bunch scallions, finely chopped

DRESSING
2 tablespoons olive oil
2 tablespoons rice vinegar
  or lemon juice
salt and pepper, to taste

ADDITIONS
grated carrot
finely chopped apple
sesame seeds
a few drops of sesame oil

1 Toss the cabbage and salt in a large bowl. Place something heavy, like a pot (any size that fits in the bowl), on top of the cabbage. The weight, along with the salt, will encourage the cabbage to expel its moisture. Leave it for 2 hours. This method will take away some bitterness, leaving the crunchy texture of raw cabbage.

2 Roast the peanuts in a single layer in a skillet over medium heat, occasionally tossing them and moving them, until they are lightly brown all over, about 5 minutes. Alternatively, spread the peanuts on a baking sheet and broil them about 2 minutes. Keep an eye on them so they don't burn. You want them nice and golden. Sprinkle a bit of salt on the roasted peanuts and set them aside.

3 Combine the olive oil, rice vinegar, salt, and pepper in a small bowl. Mix it up and taste. Adjust the salt and pepper as you like. Remember that the cabbage is already salted, so you won't need too much salt in the dressing.

4 Once the 2 hours have passed, toss the cabbage again with your hands. Cabbage treated in this way will last for several days. Before serving, add the scallions, peanuts, and dressing. Toss, taste, and adjust the seasoning as you see fit.

Broccoli Apple Salad

The bitterness of broccoli is delicious paired with the sweet tartness of apples. Plenty of crunch, too! For a slightly richer and creamier dish, try the yogurt dressing. **SERVES 4 AS A SIDE**

1 large crown and stem of broccoli

2 apples

DRESSING

juice of 1 lemon

1 tablespoon olive oil

salt and pepper, to taste

ALTERNATIVE YOGURT DRESSING

1 tablespoon yogurt

1 teaspoon olive oil

1 teaspoon lemon juice

1 teaspoon chopped fresh dill

salt and pepper, to taste

1 Slice the stem of the broccoli into ⅛-inch disks. If you can't get them that thin, don't worry, but if you have the patience, thinner is better! Once you reach the crown of the broccoli, cut the florets off and slice them as thin as you can. Set the broccoli in a bowl.

2 Halve and core the apples, then place the apples flat side down on your cutting board to make them easier to slice. Slice the apples into ⅛-inch pieces, and dump them into the bowl with the broccoli.

3 Mix the lemon juice, olive oil, salt, and pepper in a small bowl. Taste it and season with more salt and pepper as you see fit.

4 Pour the dressing over the broccoli and apples and mix it all together.

> **IF YOU PUT YOUR PLATES IN THE FRIDGE** for 10 minutes before serving, the salad will stay crisp slightly longer. For the best presentation, pile the salad as high and tight as you can manage.

SNACKS, SIDES, AND SMALL BITES

Brussels Sprout Hash and Eggs

This simple concoction is a great dish for brunch, a light lunch, or a side. The Brussels sprouts get salty and tangy from the olives and lemon, then they crisp and caramelize on the bottom. Mix in the little bit of fat from the egg yolk, and wow is this delicious. SERVES 2, OR 4 AS A SIDE

1 pound Brussels sprouts

salt and pepper, to taste

1 tablespoon butter

3 cloves garlic, finely chopped

6 olives, finely chopped

2 eggs

lemon juice, to taste

1 Chop off the ends of the sprouts. Slice them in half, then finely chop each half. Place the shreds in a bowl—you should end up with about 4 cups—and sprinkle with salt and pepper.

2 Melt the butter in a medium-size nonstick pan with a lid over medium-high heat, swirling to coat the pan. Add the Brussels sprouts and the garlic, then let them cook until just a little wilted, about 1 minute. Toss the mixture. Add the olives and toss again.

3 Crack the eggs into the pan so they aren't touching. Sprinkle with salt and pepper. Pour in 2 tablespoons water and cover with the lid. Let the eggs steam, undisturbed, until the whites are cooked through but the yolks are still runny, about 2 minutes.

4 Turn off the heat and squeeze lemon juice over everything. Serve immediately.

Mexican Street Corn

This recipe takes fresh, sweet summer corn—already amazing—and adds salt, tang, and spice to the experience. If you have an outdoor grill, prepare the corn that way, but for those without, a broiler is a great shortcut! Use any chile powder you like, such as ground ancho powder or cayenne pepper. SERVES 4 AS A SIDE

4 ears corn

4 tablespoons mayonnaise

½ cup grated cotija, queso blanco, feta, Romano, or Parmesan cheese

dusting of chile powder

1 lime, sliced into wedges

1 Turn your oven's broiler to high.

2 Peel off the corn husks and clean off all the silk. Leave the green ends attached for a convenient handhold.

3 Place the corn on a baking sheet and stick them under the broiler for 2 to 3 minutes. Rotate and repeat until they're brown and toasty all the way around—no more than 10 minutes total.

4 Working quickly, spread a tablespoon of mayonnaise over each ear of corn, lightly coating every kernel. Next, sprinkle the cheese over the corn. It should stick fairly easily to the mayonnaise, but you'll probably get a little messy.

5 Sprinkle chile powder on top, but not too heavily, or it'll be gritty.

6 Last, squeeze lime juice all over the corn, and serve hot!

My Dad's Baked Beans

My dad loves beans in basically any form. This is his formula for the quickest, easiest way to get beans on his plate without missing out on great flavor. Dad's beans rely on a can of baked beans as the base, while my version uses dried beans you might have left over from another meal. Mine requires a little more cooking and chopping to create the sauce, but it ends up less expensive because of the dried beans. Both versions taste great, so go with what works best for you: super quick and cheap, or quick and cheaper. SERVES 2, OR 4 AS A SIDE

2 teaspoons chipotle chiles in adobo with a bit of their sauce, or any chile sauce

2 cans (13.5 ounces each) baked beans

2 tablespoons mustard

2 tablespoons molasses or brown sugar

VARIATIONS

spicy mustard instead of plain

omit the chipotle

TOPPINGS

salsa

scallions

fresh cilantro

avocado

tomato

crumbled bacon

chunks of ham

1 If you're using the chipotle in adobo, chop it finely to be sure the spice will be evenly distributed.

2 Mix the chiles, beans, mustard, and molasses in a pot and place over medium heat. Cook until the beans are warmed through, 2 to 5 minutes. Give it a stir and serve. Or do it all in the microwave—that works just as well!

3 For a side dish, serve as is. To make a full meal, serve with leftover rice, over toast, in a burrito, scrambled with eggs, or stir-fried with onions and bell peppers.

And Mine

2 teaspoons chipotle chiles in adobo with a bit of their sauce, or any chile sauce

3 cups cooked pinto, red, or black beans (page 165)

½ cup pureed or chopped canned tomatoes, with juice

¼ onion, finely chopped

2 tablespoons mustard

2 tablespoons molasses or brown sugar

Cook everything in a pot over medium heat until the juices thicken, about 5 minutes. That's it!

$1.50 / **SERVING**
$3 TOTAL

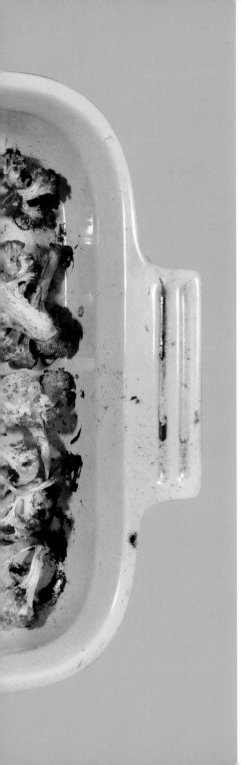

Smoky and Spicy Roasted Cauliflower

Roasted veggies are always delicious, but something magical happens to cauliflower in the oven. It gets so crispy and nutty, and that flavor is brought out even more with the spices here. I'm happy to just eat a bowl of this for dinner, maybe with an egg on top. **SERVES 4 AS A SIDE**

1 head cauliflower, stem and florets, cut into small pieces
2 cloves garlic, unpeeled
1 tablespoon butter, melted
1 teaspoon smoked paprika
½ teaspoon cayenne pepper
salt and pepper, to taste

1 Preheat the oven to 400°F.

2 Arrange the cauliflower and the garlic in a large roasting pan. Drizzle the butter over the cauliflower and sprinkle the paprika, cayenne, and generous amounts of salt and pepper over the top. Use your hands to coat the cauliflower with the butter and spices.

3 Bake until the cauliflower can be easily pierced with a fork and the florets begin to brown, 45 minutes to 1 hour. If you like things extra crispy and dark brown, bake for the full hour. To serve, squeeze the roasted garlic among the florets and trash the skins.

Crispy Chickpeas and Pumpkin Seeds

Save the seeds from your winter squash or pumpkins: Just remove them from the juicy bits inside the squash and rinse them off. Spread them out to dry on a clean surface or in an oven on its lowest setting for 15 minutes. Once dry, you can store them for several weeks. After you've built up a good supply, toast them up and enjoy! Just like with Popcorn (page 54), these are great with different spice combinations (page 149). My favorite is a half teaspoon each of ground coriander, turmeric, cumin, and cayenne pepper. SERVES 2 AS A SNACK

1½ cups cooked chickpeas, drained

½ cup pumpkin or winter squash seeds

1 teaspoon butter, melted

1 teaspoon salt

2 teaspoons any combination of ground spices (see headnote)

1 Preheat the oven to 400°F.

2 Put the chickpeas, pumpkin seeds, butter, salt, and spices in a bowl. Mix to coat every chickpea and seed with the spices.

3 Spread the chickpeas and pumpkin seeds on a baking sheet in a single layer.

4 Bake for 20 minutes.

5 Remove the baking sheet from the oven and turn the chickpeas and seeds with a spatula, making sure they aren't sticking too much. Put the baking sheet back in the oven until everything is crusty and golden, 10 more minutes.

6 Let the chickpeas and seeds cool for 10 minutes. Scoop into a bowl and serve.

Spicy Green Beans

Whenever I make these green beans, I think, "Why don't I eat this every day?" Throw a fried egg on top, serve with rice, and you have a delicious meal. Try to find the chile paste called *sambal oelek*; it's commonly available and you'll love having it in your flavor arsenal. It's my favorite Asian chile paste for this dish. It has a lovely, pure flavor, and (usually) no added vinegar or garlic. SERVES 2 AS A SIDE

$0.65 / SERVING
$1.30 TOTAL

1 teaspoon vegetable oil

8 ounces green beans, ends trimmed and chopped into bite-size pieces

2 cloves garlic, finely chopped

1 teaspoon soy sauce

1 teaspoon sambal oelek

ADDITIONS

1 teaspoon grated ginger

1 teaspoon lemon juice

1 Place a frying pan over medium heat and add the vegetable oil. Once it's hot, add the green beans. Let them cook undisturbed for about 1 minute.

2 Mix the garlic, soy sauce, sambal oelek, and any additions in a small bowl. This is your sauce!

3 After 1 minute, the beans should have turned bright green. Add about ¼ cup of water to the pan. Cook for another 2 minutes, until the water is mostly gone.

4 Pour the sauce into the pan and toss gently to coat. Cook until everything is fragrant and most of the liquid is gone, another 2 minutes. Poke the beans with a fork: If it goes through easily, they're done.

5 Add more chile sauce or soy sauce to taste if you want the beans hotter or saltier.

ideas

POPCORN!

Popcorn is such a great snack. It's easy to forget how simple and cheap it is to prepare at home when there are so many prepackaged varieties available at ten times the price.

It's also fun to get kids involved since the transformation is so dramatic and explosive. Science! Make the popcorn your own by adding your favorite flavors to it. My family went for Parmesan and black pepper on Sunday nights when I was growing up.

Be sure to experiment and figure out what suits you best. I've suggested a few toppings on the opposite page. This recipe makes 10 to 12 cups of popped popcorn—enough for four people. Eat it while it's hot!

Basic Popcorn

SERVES 4 AS A SNACK

2 tablespoons vegetable oil

⅓ cup unpopped popcorn kernels

2 tablespoons butter, melted

salt, to taste

1 Place a large pot with a tight-fitting lid on the stove. Pour in the vegetable oil, then the popcorn kernels. Put the lid on and turn the heat to medium.

2 Using oven mitts, gently shake the pot from side to side to make sure the kernels are evenly distributed in the oil. Once the popcorn begins to pop, turn the heat down to medium low and shake again.

3 Once the popping slows to 5 to 10 seconds between pops, turn off the heat. Wait until you're sure the popping has stopped, and remove the lid.

4 Dump the popcorn into a large bowl, pour the butter over the top, and sprinkle with salt and any other toppings. Gently toss to coat.

1. Minced scallion and cilantro
2. Turmeric and coriander
3. Spice Oil (page 151)
4. Parmesan and black pepper
5. Cayenne pepper and smoked paprika
6. Brown sugar and orange zest
7. Chili powder and lime
8. Parmesan and dried oregano

Mashed Beets

Making a mash or puree out of beets is a little different than making a mash out of another kind of root. Beets are much less starchy, so they don't naturally fluff up as much as other winter vegetables. For the smoothest results, use a food processor. The puree is electric magenta and delicious (although it's just as good when chunky). **SERVES 4 AS A SIDE**

salt, to taste

4 medium-size beets

1 tablespoon butter

3 cloves garlic, finely chopped

¼ cup chicken or vegetable broth

pepper, to taste

ADDITIONS

orange juice instead of broth

dill

yogurt or sour cream

vinegar

1 Bring a pot of salted water to a boil. Add the beets, in their skins, and cook until a knife can pierce them easily, about 40 minutes.

2 Drain the water and let the beets cool for 5 minutes.

3 Meanwhile, melt the butter in a pan over medium heat. Sauté the garlic until it smells great and turns translucent, but not brown, about 2 minutes. Remove from the heat and set aside.

4 Once the beets are cool, chop off the tough stems and peel off the skin. It should be quite easy, because the cooking will have softened the exterior.

5 Dice the beets and add them to a bowl or a food processor, along with the sautéed garlic, the broth, and any additions. Process or mash until the mixture is very smooth. Taste and add salt and pepper as needed.

Mashed Cauliflower

Mashed cauliflower has a very light, nutty taste that soaks up the flavors you add to it, much like potatoes. Unlike potatoes, it's lighter in your belly and more interesting in texture. SERVES 4 AS A SIDE

salt, to taste

1 head cauliflower, chopped

1 tablespoon butter

3 cloves garlic, finely chopped

pepper, to taste

ADDITIONS

spices (page 149)

grated cheese

yogurt or sour cream

chiles, finely chopped

ginger, finely grated

scallions, chopped

1 Bring a large pot of salted water to a boil. Add the cauliflower and cook until tender, 5 to 7 minutes.

2 Drain the water and remove the cauliflower.

3 Place the pot back over medium heat and add the butter. Let it melt, add the garlic, and sauté for about 2 minutes. Put the cauliflower back into the pot. Stir to coat, and cook until it is just heated through, or for a little longer to let it get golden and crispy. Your choice!

4 Turn off the heat and let the mixture cool for 5 minutes. Use a potato masher to smash the cauliflower roughly. Add salt, pepper, and any other additions, and mash and mix some more. Taste and adjust as desired.

Winter Squash Puree

The easiest way to cook winter squash is to roast it whole. The inside becomes soft and smooth and you can scoop it out of the skin with ease.

SERVES 4 AS A SIDE

1 tablespoon butter, plus more for the pan

1 butternut, kabocha, acorn, delicata, or other winter squash (except spaghetti squash)

3 cloves garlic

salt and pepper, to taste

ADDITIONS

yogurt or sour cream

brown sugar and cinnamon

finely chopped chiles

curry powder

raisins

sage

1 Preheat the oven to 400°F. Butter a baking sheet.

2 Slice the squash in half using a big, sharp knife. Scoop out the innards. Set the halves facedown on the sheet.

3 Bake in the oven until a knife poked into the squash goes through easily, 30 to 40 minutes.

4 Melt the butter in a pan over medium heat. Add the garlic and sauté about 2 minutes. Remove from the heat.

5 Scoop the squash into a large bowl with the garlic, the butter from the pan, and any other additions. Stir until smooth. Taste and add salt and pepper as needed.

Mashed Celery Root

Celery root is just what it sounds like. It's the root from which the stalks of celery grow, and yes, you can eat it! Knobbly and ugly as it may appear, it tastes as if a potato and celery had a baby. **SERVES 4 AS A SIDE**

salt, to taste

1 medium-size celery root, peeled and diced

1 tablespoon butter

3 cloves garlic

½ cup broth or water, warm

pepper, to taste

ADDITIONS

chopped fresh cilantro

grated ginger

yogurt or sour cream

chile flakes

1 Bring a pot of salted water to a boil.

2 Add the celery root to the pot and let the water return to a boil. Reduce the heat to a simmer and cook until the celery root is easy to pierce with a fork, 20 minutes. Drain the water and put the celery root in a bowl.

3 Place the pot back over medium heat and add the butter. Let it melt, add the garlic, and sauté until fragrant, about 2 minutes. Put the celery root back in the pot. Stir to coat, and cook until the celery root begins to get a bit mushy, about 5 minutes.

4 Turn off the heat and add the broth along with any other additions. Use a potato masher, food processor, or electric mixer to smash the celery root until smooth. (Get it smooth enough and you'll almost think it's a potato.) Season with salt and pepper to taste.

method
BUBBLE AND SQUEAK

Bubble and Squeak is a traditional British weekend breakfast food meant to use up the leftovers from the night before. Because it's British, of course the recipe includes mashed potatoes! It's basically a big potato pancake with stuff mixed into it. Chop up any other stray vegetables you have lying around. Find a carrot? Grate it or finely chop it and add it to the bowl. Cabbage, peas, corn, broccoli, Brussels sprouts—all these things are great. You won't want to add really watery vegetables like tomato, zucchini, or cucumber, though, so stick to precooked or tougher ones.

The adorable name comes from the sound this dish makes in the pan, the squeak coming from the cabbage, which is the most common mix-in for the potato. The method I'm giving you is for one big pancake, but you could make smaller pancakes for a neater presentation. You can also forget the pancakes entirely and make a hash out of the mixture. This method is more of a technique than a traditional recipe, so just try to embrace the concept: Crispy and hot, you can't go wrong!

2 cups mashed potatoes

1 cup mashed root vegetables (pages 57 to 60) or roasted vegetables (page 106)

salt and pepper, to taste

1 tablespoon butter

ADDITIONS

½ cup peas

½ cup cabbage

2 to 3 scallions, finely chopped

1 Combine the mashed potatoes and mashed root vegetables or roasted vegetables in a large bowl. The above measurements are a general guideline, but you can tweak the ratios so long as you have enough potato to hold it all together. (If it's falling apart, add more potato!)

2 Sprinkle with salt and pepper and mix everything together into a big thick kind of dough. Taste it and see if it needs more salt and pepper. Since you are using leftovers that are already seasoned, you probably won't need to add much salt. This may seem haphazard, but it's a very forgiving recipe and as long as the mixture is at least half mashed potato it should work out just fine.

3 Melt the butter in a cast-iron or nonstick skillet over medium heat. **Add the mixture to the pan and press it into a flat pancake** that fills the pan all the way to the edge. Let it cook for 5 to 7 minutes without touching it.

4 Use a spatula to check the underside of the pancake. **When it's golden, it's time to flip it.** (If it's not, wait another minute or two.) Now comes a decision. You can try to flip the pancake all in one go—something I usually fail at—or you can simply flip it bit by bit. No need to worry if you break it up. After you flip the pancake, squish it back together again with the spatula. Brown the other side of the pancake for another 10 minutes. Once you have a nice golden crust around the whole pancake, turn off the heat. Let cool in the pan for 10 minutes.

5 Slice into wedges to serve.

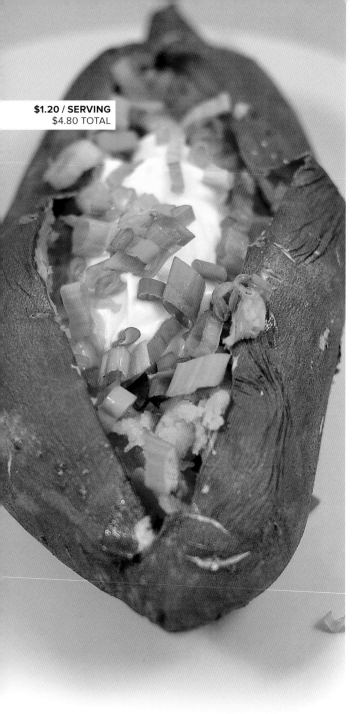

Jacket Sweet Potatoes

I like to serve these with all kinds of toppings, usually leftovers from other meals. Try filling them with roasted chicken, beans and cheese, corn and tomatoes—whatever you have around (but avoid veggies that can't stand up to residual heat, like lettuce or cucumbers). SERVES 4

4 large sweet potatoes
salt and pepper, to taste
¼ cup sour cream
½ bunch scallions, finely chopped

1 Preheat the oven to 400°F.

2 Scrub the sweet potatoes and stab them with a fork a few times. Lay them on a baking sheet.

3 Bake for 60 to 75 minutes. Because sweet potatoes vary greatly in size, stick them with a long knife after an hour to check them. If it goes through easily, they're ready. If not, bake longer.

4 Let the potatoes cool for 15 minutes. Make a long cut along the top of each potato and open them gently. Beat the soft, orange middle with a fork to fluff it up.

5 Sprinkle with salt and pepper. Let each person add sour cream and scallions (or more salt and pepper) to their taste.

Roasted Potatoes with Chiles

It doesn't get much simpler or more satisfying than roasted potatoes. You can use any pepper you like—from large, dark poblanos to Hungarian wax chiles to bell peppers. When you chop the peppers, be sure to get rid of the seeds and white ribs inside. In addition to being a great side dish, this makes a delicious taco filling. Alternatively, try it alongside some black beans and rice or piled high on a plate with an egg on top. SERVES 4 AS A SIDE

4 medium-size potatoes, chopped into bite-size pieces

4 medium-size chile peppers or 2 bell peppers, chopped into bite-size pieces

2 cloves garlic, unpeeled

1 tablespoon butter, melted

salt and pepper, to taste

1 Preheat the oven to 400°F.

2 Tumble the potatoes, peppers, and garlic together in a large roasting pan.

3 Pour the butter over the top and sprinkle liberally with salt and pepper. Potatoes need quite a bit of salt! Use your hands to mix everything up.

4 Roast until you can spear the potatoes easily with a fork and everything is a little crispy, about 1 hour. Squish the garlic cloves, spread the roasted garlic throughout, and discard the skins.

Poutine

Poutine, a French-Canadian dish of French fries, gravy, and cheese curds, isn't an everyday meal, but it's a favorite. Since I don't like deep-frying at home, I bake the fries—they still get crispy without the fuss. Montreal-style poutine is made with vegetable gravy, as in this recipe, but you can also use beef or turkey gravy. Of course, proper poutine uses cheese curds, and if you can find them do use them, but fresh mozzarella works almost as well. It has the same spongy quality, just maybe with a little less squeak. However, using fresh mozzarella makes this recipe come out a little more on the expensive side than you would think. If you use less or skip the cheese entirely, you can cut the price in half. **SERVES 4 AS A SIDE**

---

2 tablespoons vegetable oil

2 to 3 medium russet potatoes, cut into sticks

salt and pepper, to taste

6 ounces fresh mozzarella cheese, diced

1 to 2 scallions, chopped

GRAVY

2 tablespoons butter

1 shallot or 3 scallions, finely chopped

3 cloves garlic, finely chopped

6 leaves fresh sage, finely chopped (optional)

2 tablespoons all-purpose flour

1½ cups vegetable broth

1 teaspoon soy sauce

½ teaspoon cayenne pepper

salt and pepper, to taste

1 Preheat the oven to 400°F.

2 Spread 1 tablespoon of the vegetable oil on a baking sheet, then add the potato. Drizzle the remaining tablespoon of oil over the potatoes and sprinkle them generously with salt and pepper. Toss the potatoes with your hands and evenly space them across the baking sheet. Bake for 20 minutes.

3 Meanwhile, melt the butter in a small saucepan over medium heat. Swirl it around to coat the pan. Add the shallot, garlic, and sage, if using, and cook until the shallots are translucent but not brown, about 2 minutes. Quickly stir in the flour. Add a little vegetable broth if the mixture gets too lumpy.

4 Let the mixture cook until it turns light brown. Add the vegetable broth, soy sauce, and cayenne pepper. Bring the gravy to a boil, then turn down the heat and let it cook until it thickens to a gravy-ish consistency, about 5 minutes, stirring occasionally. Taste it, adding salt and pepper as needed. Turn down the heat to its lowest setting, just enough to keep the gravy warm.

5 After the fries have baked for 20 minutes, remove them from the oven. Shuffle them with a spatula and test with a fork. If it goes through easily, the fries are ready. If you want them a little crispier, flip them over and put them back in the oven for a bit.

6 Once they're done, pile one layer of fries onto a plate. Top with the diced mozzarella and the gravy. Repeat with a second layer and sprinkle with scallions and more freshly ground black pepper.

$1.75 / SERVING
$7 TOTAL

ideas
THINGS ON TOAST

I love bread, and toast in particular is my comfort food. Here, I suggest that you take some toast and put something tasty on it. That's it!

I like these recipes for times when I'm on my own and want a quick meal or snack. They're a great way to use leftovers or turn a side dish into a full meal. What makes this more like a special dinner than a quick snack is the way you treat the bread—toasting it in the pan like a nice piece of fish.

A pile of sautéed or raw veggies over buttered, crusty toast is the perfect meal for one or two and a great way to try a new vegetable. I've suggested a few topping variations on the following pages, but you can use pretty much any veggie dish from this book or invent your own. Go with raw vegetable salads or, as I most often do, sauté veggies or cooked beans in oil with flavors like garlic and chiles, olives and dill, ginger and turmeric, or any other classic combination (page 149). It only takes a few minutes, and the result is an aromatic, attractive, satisfying meal.

Basic Toast

SERVES 2

4 slices bread

2 tablespoons butter

salt and pepper, to taste

2 fried eggs (optional)

1 Melt ½ tablespoon of the butter in a pan over medium heat. Place 2 slices of bread in the pan, let them cook for about 2 minutes, then lift them with a spatula to see if they're golden brown underneath. When they are, flip 'em over.

2 Add another ½ tablespoon of the butter to the pan to make sure the second side of the toast becomes just as golden as the first. Sprinkle the toast with salt and pepper. Once the second side is golden, set the bread on a plate to await its topping. Repeat with the remaining bread and butter.

3 Pile on some toppings (see the following pages for inspiration) and finish each with a fried egg, if you have it.

❶ Peas and Lemon

$1 SERVING / $2 TOTAL

A less salty, more rustic version of the British classic mushy peas.

1 teaspoon olive oil
2 cloves garlic, finely chopped
1 cup peas, fresh or frozen
1 teaspoon lemon juice
freshly grated Romano or Parmesan cheese
salt and pepper, to taste

Place a pan on the stove over medium heat and add the olive oil. Drop in the garlic and peas along with 2 tablespoons water so that the peas can steam a bit. Leave them until they turn bright green. Sprinkle with the lemon juice, cheese, salt, and pepper, then remove the peas from the heat and mash with the back of a fork, either in the pan or in a bowl. Pile onto warm toast and enjoy!

❷ Asian Greens Gra Prow

$2.50 SERVING / $5 TOTAL

Try any Asian green you can get your hands on, from bok choy to tatsoi to gai lan. *Gra prow* means stir-fried with Thai basil.

1 teaspoon vegetable oil
2 cloves garlic, chopped
1 teaspoon grated ginger
2 teaspoons soy sauce
1 bunch Asian greens, stems and leaves chopped separately
1 handful Thai basil
salt and pepper, to taste

Heat the oil in a pan over medium heat. Sauté the garlic until fragrant, 2 minutes, then add the ginger, soy sauce, and the chopped stems of the greens. Cook until almost tender, 4 to 5 minutes. Add the rest of the greens and cook for 2 more minutes. Turn off the heat and mix in the Thai basil, salt, and pepper.

❸ Caramelized Onions and Cheddar

$1 SERVING / $2 TOTAL

Caramelizing onions isn't quick, but if you make a large batch it's worth it. Sweet onion and salty Cheddar are a drool-inducing pair!

1 tablespoon butter
1 red onion, thinly sliced
sharp Cheddar cheese, thinly sliced
salt and pepper, to taste

Melt the butter in a pan over low heat. Add the onion and cook slowly, about 20 minutes. As the onions darken, stir occasionally, adding water to loosen the sticky bits. When the onions are sweet and caramelized, spread them over toast, and top with Cheddar, salt, and pepper. Put the toast back in the pan and cook, covered, until the cheese is bubbly.

❹ Roasted Vegetables

$1 SERVING / $2 TOTAL

One of my favorite ways to eat leftover roasted vegetables.

Roasted Vegetables (page 106)
freshly grated Romano or Parmesan cheese
pepper, to taste

Simply create a ridiculously tall pile of vegetables like the winter squash and leeks pictured here, then sprinkle with grated Romano and fresh pepper. You can also add any sauce you have on hand, or sprinkle crushed nuts on top.

❺ Salty Broccoli

$1.50 SERVING / $3 TOTAL

Most broccoli that enters my home meets its fate as this dish.

1 teaspoon olive oil
3 cloves garlic, chopped
1 teaspoon chile flakes
1 anchovy fillet, chopped
1 crown and stem of broccoli, chopped
freshly grated Romano or Parmesan cheese
salt and pepper, to taste

Warm the oil in a pan over medium heat. Add the garlic and chile flakes and cook 2 minutes. Add the anchovy and cook for another minute. Add the broccoli and ¼ cup water. Cover the pan, steam for 3 minutes, then toss and cook for 2 minutes, until the broccoli is tender and the water is gone. Spoon onto warm toast. Top with cheese, salt, and pepper.

❻ Broiled Eggplant Salad

$1.75 SERVING / $3.50 TOTAL

Yet another use for leftovers—or just a way to make a great salad more substantial.

Broiled Eggplant Salad (page 32)
chopped fresh herbs or greens
any cheese, crumbled or grated

Simply dollop the Broiled Eggplant Salad onto toast, then add some herbs or greens to the top for a fresh counterpoint, along with a bit of cheese.

❼ Peas and Collards

$1 SERVING / $2 TOTAL

Oh man, is there anything more comforting than beans (or these bean-like peas) on toast? Everyone will be delighted even if you're just using up leftovers. To make the meal a little more fancy, use scones instead of toast.

Black-Eyed Peas and Collards (page 111)
Whole-Wheat Jalapeño Cheddar Scones (page 15)

Heat up the peas and collards in a pan on the stovetop or simply in the microwave. Spoon over warm toast and enjoy. If you're using the scones, slice them in half and toast them in a toaster oven or under your broiler before dolloping each half with the pea mixture.

❽ Spinach and Chickpea

$4.50 SERVING / $2.25 TOTAL

A popular tapas dish in Spain. This recipe makes a little more topping than you need for four pieces of toast—but hey, leftovers are tasty.

1 teaspoon butter
2 cloves garlic, chopped
1 cup cooked chickpeas
1 bunch spinach, washed, thicker stems removed
salt and pepper, to taste
smoked paprika (optional)

Melt the butter in a pan on medium heat. Add the garlic and cook for 2 minutes. Add the chickpeas and spinach, then cook for 2 to 5 minutes, until the spinach cooks down but is still bright green. Taste and add salt and pepper, then spoon over warm toast. If you have it, sprinkle with smoked paprika.

9 Avocado

$0.90 SERVING / $1.80 TOTAL

Years ago, my partner and I arrived in Sydney, Australia, after cycling hundreds of miles. Our hosts gave us a mountain of toast with avocado. I may have eaten an entire loaf of bread and maybe three avocados. It is one of the most memorable meals of my life.

1 avocado
salt and pepper, to taste
chile flakes (optional)
lemon or lime wedge
  (optional)

Slice the avocado and remove the pit—it should pop out easily. Scoop the avocado flesh out of each side, and slice in half again so you have 4 equal portions. Mash the avocado with a fork and spread onto the toast. Top with salt and pepper, a few chile flakes, and a squeeze of lemon or lime juice, if using.

10 Apple Cheddar

$1.40 SERVING / $2.80 TOTAL

Have you ever seen anyone eat apple pie with a little Cheddar on it? This is the same, but even better! Try using an aged white Cheddar if you can get it, but your favorite standard Cheddar will do just as well. Crisp apple plus luscious, salty, crumbly Cheddar equals one of my favorite late-night snacks (even minus the toast).

2 ounces Cheddar cheese
1 apple
salt and pepper, to taste

Thinly slice the Cheddar and slice the apple. I prefer to layer the apples and then slide small slices of Cheddar in between them, but do it in whatever way makes sense to you.

11 Sautéed Mushrooms

$1.75 SERVING / $3.50 TOTAL

Rich and earthy, the smell of mushrooms and garlic will have neighbors knocking on your door. These are also an incredible hamburger topping, so consider making enough for leftovers.

1 tablespoon butter
1 pound mushrooms,
  sliced
4 cloves garlic, chopped
salt and pepper, to taste

Melt the butter in a pan over medium heat. Add the mushrooms and sauté until they have shrunk and expelled some of their liquid, about 2 minutes. Mix in the garlic and cook until the mushrooms are light brown all over, about 5 more minutes. Add salt and pepper to taste. Spoon onto warm toast.

12 Korean-Style Spinach

$1.75 SERVING / $3.50 TOTAL

This spinach, sautéed with sesame and garlic, is one of my favorites.

1 teaspoon olive oil
4 cloves garlic, chopped
1 bunch spinach, washed,
  thicker stems removed
1 teaspoon soy sauce
½ teaspoon toasted
  sesame oil
salt, to taste
1 teaspoon sesame seeds

Heat the olive oil in a pan over medium heat. Add the garlic and cook, 2 minutes. Add the spinach and soy sauce and cook for 2 minutes, until the spinach has wilted and shrunk. Turn off the heat and add the sesame oil and salt. Mix and taste. Remove the spinach from the pan and squeeze out any excess moisture. Serve over hot slices of toast. Sprinkle sesame seeds on top.

method
CORNMEAL-CRUSTED VEGGIES

These are kind of like veggie French fries. The cornmeal makes them super crunchy, and they're great with a dipping sauce. Might I suggest Peanut Sauce (page 143)? Almost any vegetable works well with this method—some of my favorites are zucchini wedges, bell pepper strips, and wedges of cooked winter squash. (Pictured are bell peppers and green beans.) It's sort of like fried green tomatoes or okra, but this baked version skips the expense and mess of the oil while keeping the crunch.

oil or butter, for the baking sheet

½ cup all-purpose flour

2 eggs

¼ cup milk

1 cup cornmeal

1 teaspoon salt

1 teaspoon black pepper

1 teaspoon paprika

½ teaspoon garlic powder

8 ounces green beans, stemmed

VARIATIONS

zucchini wedges

bell pepper strips

cooked winter squash wedges

cauliflower florets

broccoli florets

whole okra

carrot or parsnip sticks

asparagus, whole if very thin

1 **Preheat the oven to 450°F.**

2 **Grease a baking sheet** with a small amount of oil or butter.

3 **Set up your breading station!** Spread the flour on a plate. Crack both eggs into a bowl, add the milk, and beat lightly with a fork. On another plate, spread the cornmeal, salt, black pepper, paprika, and garlic powder, and mix them up with your fingers.

4 A few at a time, **dredge the green beans in the flour and transfer them to the egg mixture.** Coat the beans lightly with the egg, being careful to shake off any excess. Then **transfer to the cornmeal mixture** and coat them evenly.

5 **Spread the veggies on the baking sheet.** Repeat until you've done them all. If you run out of any of the three mixtures, just mix up a bit more.

6 **Bake for 10 to 15 minutes,** until golden and crispy. Enjoy hot with your favorite dipping sauce!

Green Chile and Cheddar Quesadillas

These are a great snack or a quick meal, and you can add pretty much anything to them! To make 'em cheaper, use fresh tortillas made from scratch (page 155). **SERVES 2**

4 Tortillas (page 155)

½ cup chopped green chiles, canned or fresh

½ cup grated sharp Cheddar cheese

1 tablespoon chopped fresh cilantro

TO SERVE

Salsa (page 145), for serving

sour cream, for serving

1 Place 1 tortilla on a cutting board and spread half of the green chiles evenly over the top. Sprinkle half of the cheese over the chiles, then top with half the cilantro. Place another tortilla on top of each prepared tortilla to form a quesadilla. Repeat!

2 Place a large, nonstick pan over medium heat. Once it's hot, add a quesadilla and toast until the tortilla browns, about 1 minute. Flip it over and brown the second side, then do the same for the other quesadilla. Slice into triangles and enjoy with some fresh salsa and sour cream.

Filipino Chicken Adobo

This ultra-adaptable recipe comes to us courtesy of Tony Pangilinan, who grew up on food stamps after his family immigrated from the Philippines "with nothing but four suitcases and a lot of dreams." After several decades of struggle, Tony achieved those dreams and can now help family members who remain in poverty in the Philippines. He says that, despite their hard circumstances, his family still feels blessed.

Filipino adobo—very different from Spanish adobo—is basically anything cooked in vinegar, soy sauce, and garlic. Although this version is made with chicken, you can use any meat or vegetables you like. Because it's vinegar-based, it keeps well in the fridge! SERVES 8

---

8 chicken thighs

¾ cup rice vinegar or distilled white vinegar

¼ cup soy sauce

2 cloves garlic, minced

½ teaspoon black pepper

2 bay leaves

2 tablespoons vegetable oil

2 medium-size potatoes, chopped

4 medium-size carrots, sliced

2 cups white rice

2 pinches of salt

2 teaspoons cornstarch mixed with 1 tablespoon water

ADDITIONS

4 jalapeño peppers, sliced (remove seeds for less heat)

ginger, grated

VARIATIONS

1½ pounds pork shoulder or butt

substitute 1 can (13.5 ounces) coconut milk for the water

1 Cut off the chicken fat. Don't get rid of every last bit, just trim what seems excessive.

2 Stir together the vinegar, soy sauce, garlic, pepper, and bay leaves in a large, non-aluminum pan. Add the chicken, coating each piece. Cover and marinate for 30 minutes (overnight is great).

3 Remove the chicken from the marinade and pat each piece dry with paper towels. (Don't throw out the marinade! You'll use it later.)

4 Pour the oil into a large pot over medium heat. Once it's hot, add enough chicken to cover the bottom. Cook until one side of the chicken is browned, just a few minutes, then flip it over and repeat. When the first batch of chicken is done, remove it from the pot and repeat.

5 After all the chicken is browned, put it back in the pot along with the marinade, potatoes, carrots, and ¾ cup of water. Turn the heat up, bring the liquid to a boil, then decrease the heat to low. Simmer until the meat is cooked through and the carrots and potatoes are soft, about 45 minutes. Cut into the meat. If it's no longer pink, it's done.

6 When the dish is almost ready, pour the rice into a medium-size pot with 4 cups of water and the salt. Bring to a boil over medium heat. Turn the heat down and cover with a lid placed slightly askew. Cook until the water is gone, about 20 minutes.

7 Remove the bay leaves from the adobo and stir in the cornstarch and water mixture. Let it thicken until the chicken and vegetables are well glazed. Serve over the rice.

Roast Chicken

Although chicken ranges widely in prices, a whole chicken is usually less expensive than buying single pieces like breasts or thighs—plus you can make broth later from the bones and any meat too difficult to get off. The leftovers can be used in sandwiches, in tacos, over a salad, or tossed with sauce and mixed into pasta. This is a base recipe: Add spices to the butter or sprinkle them over the surface of the chicken to change up the flavor in any way you like. SERVES 6

1 whole chicken, about 4 pounds
1 tablespoon butter, melted
salt and pepper, to taste
2 cloves garlic
1 lemon

1 Preheat the oven to 400°F.

2 Remove the giblets from the inside of the chicken and chop off the neck. Keep them for broth later. You can either freeze them or just leave them in the fridge if you plan to make broth in the next couple of days. Rub the entire bird with the melted butter, then sprinkle it with salt and pepper.

3 Smash the garlic cloves with the side of a knife blade, remove the peel, and slice the lemon in half. Stuff the garlic and lemon into the body cavity.

4 Place the chicken in a roasting pan or an ovenproof skillet. Transfer to the oven and cook for 1 hour. If you have a meat thermometer, check to make sure the chicken is at 165°F, the temperature at which chicken is completely safe to eat, but an hour in a 400°F oven should be long enough to cook it fully.

5 Let the chicken rest for at least 10 minutes before you carve it to make sure you don't lose any of the tasty juices. Remove the garlic and lemon before carving.

AFTER YOU CARVE AWAY all the meat, make chicken broth from the carcass, giblets, and neck. Simmer them for several hours in a pot full of water along with vegetable scraps like the ends of onions and carrots, plus a generous helping of salt.

Peanut Chicken and Broccoli with Coconut Rice

This recipe uses peanut sauce to elevate a pretty plain chicken and broccoli stir-fry to something you'll want to serve to your favorite guests. Make a full batch of the Peanut Sauce (page 143) and use some for this and the rest for dipping veggies, dressing salads, or smothering your favorite protein. **SERVES 6**

1½ cups long-grain rice

1 can (13.5 ounces) coconut milk

½ teaspoon salt, plus more to taste

1½ pounds chicken (any part), chopped into bite-size pieces

pepper, to taste

2 teaspoons vegetable oil

6 cups chopped broccoli, stems and florets separated (about 1 large bunch)

½ cup Peanut Sauce (page 143)

chopped fresh cilantro

VARIATION

10 ounces tofu, cut into cubes and marinated in ¼ cup soy sauce, instead of chicken

1 Rinse the rice. Add it, along with the coconut milk, salt, and 1½ cups water, to a pot over medium heat. Bring to a boil, then turn the heat to low. Let the rice simmer, covered, with the lid askew, until the liquid is gone, about 20 minutes. If the rice is done before the stir-fry, remove it from the heat, fluff it a bit with a fork so it doesn't stick to the pot, and cover to keep it warm.

2 While the rice cooks, sprinkle the chicken with salt and pepper and set aside.

3 Place a large pan or wok over medium-high heat and add 1 teaspoon of the vegetable oil. Let it get hot and add the broccoli stems. Cook, stirring occasionally, to soften the stems, about 3 minutes. Add the tops of the broccoli and ¼ cup of water and cover the pan. It will steam and sizzle a lot, so watch out! Let the broccoli cook until the water evaporates, about 3 more minutes. Test a piece of broccoli with a fork. It

should be just barely tender, but not soft. Turn off the heat and remove the broccoli from the pan.

4 Add the remaining teaspoon of oil to the pan and put it back over medium heat. Add the chicken and cook, stirring occasionally, until it's no longer pink, about 5 minutes. Add another ¼ cup water and stir occasionally until the chicken is cooked all the way through, another 2 minutes.

5 Add the peanut sauce and stir to coat the chicken. Don't worry if the sauce seems too thick at first. It will blend with the water to become a glaze.

6 Once the chicken is coated with sauce, put the broccoli back into the pan and stir it all together. Taste and add salt as needed.

7 Scoop the coconut rice onto plates and top with the broccoli, chicken, and cilantro.

Beef Stroganoff

Beef stroganoff is one of my husband's favorites, so I make it as a treat for him—and one of my early readers, Dave, says his mother made it for him growing up. It's a classic winter meal from Eastern Europe that warms up a cold house and fills the air with rich aromas. You can use any cut of beef, but adjust the cooking time based on the toughness. If you aren't sure about which cuts of beef to use here, ask your butcher. SERVES 6

1 pound beef chuck or other cut

salt and pepper, to taste

2 tablespoons butter

2 onions, chopped

2 large carrots, chopped

1 tablespoon flour

2 teaspoons paprika

1 pound egg noodles or any pasta

3 cloves garlic, finely chopped

1 pound mushrooms, chopped

½ cup sour cream

3 tablespoons mustard

ADDITIONS

½ cup red wine (add with the water in Step 3)

potatoes and 1 bell pepper, chopped (add with the carrots and onions in Step 3)

fresh dill (for garnish)

1 Chop the raw beef into bite-size pieces and season them generously with salt and pepper.

2 Melt 1 tablespoon of the butter in a large saucepan over medium heat. Toss in enough beef to cover the bottom of the pan. You may need to cook the meat in two batches, depending on the size of your pan. Brown the meat on all sides, then set it aside on a plate.

3 Add the onions and carrots to the pan and cook until the onions become translucent. Sprinkle the flour and paprika over the top, then cover everything with 4 cups of water. Put the meat back into the pot. Place a lid slightly askew on the pot so steam can escape. Let cook over medium-low heat until the beef is tender and the water has turned into broth, about 2 hours.

4 Bring a large pot of salted water to a boil. Cook the noodles according to the package instructions. Try to time it to coincide with finishing the stew.

5 Meanwhile, melt the remaining tablespoon of butter in another pan over medium heat. Add the garlic and cook until fragrant, about a minute. Add the mushrooms, toss them to coat, sprinkle with salt and pepper, and cook, stirring occasionally, until they shrink and turn brown, about 5 minutes. Turn off the heat, taste, and add salt and pepper as needed.

6 Check on the beef. If the water has reduced to about a cup of thick, flavorful liquid and the beef is tender, it's done! If not, let it cook a little longer and keep checking on it. Once it's ready, turn down the heat and stir in the mushrooms, sour cream, and mustard. Taste and add more salt, pepper, and paprika if needed.

7 Serve the stew over the noodles and sprinkle with more paprika.

IF YOU'RE USING A PRICIER, MORE TENDER CUT OF BEEF, like round steak or sirloin tip, you don't need to cook it nearly as long. Simply brown the meat, substitute 1 cup of beef broth for the water, and cook for 20 to 30 minutes.

Spicy Broiled Tilapia with Lime

This meal comes together so quickly it's astonishing. Broiled fish is crispy on the outside and flaky and moist on the inside. Serve with rice, a vegetable mash (see pages 57 to 60), or a favorite side dish like Spicy Green Beans (page 53). If you sauté some vegetables while the fish cooks, dinner will be on the table in minutes. SERVES 2

1 teaspoon vegetable oil

1 teaspoon salt

½ teaspoon black pepper

1 teaspoon cayenne pepper

1 teaspoon ground cumin

½ teaspoon garlic powder

½ teaspoon dried oregano

2 fillets tilapia or other white fish

½ lime

1 Turn your oven's broiler to high. Line a baking sheet with aluminum foil and coat it evenly with the vegetable oil to keep the fish from sticking.

2 In a small bowl, mix together the salt, pepper, cayenne, cumin, garlic powder, and oregano. Sprinkle them over both sides of the fish and massage gently with your fingers until the fish is covered thoroughly.

3 Place the fish on the prepared baking pan. If you are using a fillet that still has its skin, make sure it is skin-side up so it will get crispy.

4 Broil the fillets for 4 to 7 minutes. The fish will cook very quickly, so check after 4 minutes by gently

inserting a butter knife into the thickest part. If it goes through easily and the fish flakes apart, then it's done. If the knife meets resistance and the fish stays together, put the fillets back under the broiler for another few minutes. Once you've made this recipe once or twice, you'll be able to tell at a glance when your fish is done.

5 When the fish is done, squeeze lime juice over it.

> **SOME BROILERS** are not strong enough to get the skin crispy—if that's the case for you, pull it off just before serving. Or leave it. Crispy or not, fish skin is delicious.

Creamy Zucchini Fettuccine

Zucchini and summer squash are so abundant in the summer months. This simple pasta is like a lighter, brighter fettuccine alfredo. It also comes together in no time—the veggies will be ready by the time your pasta is cooked. You'll love it, I promise. **SERVES 3, OR 2 VERY HUNGRY PEOPLE**

---

salt, to taste

8 ounces fettuccine

4 tablespoons butter

4 cloves garlic, finely chopped

½ teaspoon chile flakes

2 small zucchini, finely diced

zest of 1 lemon

¼ cup heavy cream

½ cup grated Romano or Parmesan cheese

pepper, to taste

sprinkling of finely chopped fresh basil (optional)

1 Bring a pot of water to a boil over high heat. Salt the water liberally. This is how pasta gets its flavor, so don't be shy! Most of the salt won't end up in the pasta.

2 Cook the pasta according to the package directions. I drain the pasta just before it's finished so it doesn't get mushy when I add it to the vegetable pan and it gets cooked a little more.

3 Meanwhile, melt 1 tablespoon of the butter in a pan over medium heat. Add the garlic and chile flakes. Let them sizzle for 30 seconds to a minute, then add the zucchini. Stir the vegetables to coat. Cook, stirring occasionally, until some of the water has cooked off and the veggies are tender, 5 to 7 minutes. Young summer zucchini doesn't need much cooking. Add the lemon zest. Stir!

4 Drain the fettuccine and add it to the pan along with the remaining 3 tablespoons of butter, the cream, and most of the cheese. Toss the fettuccine around the pan, and add salt and lots of freshly ground pepper to taste. Top with a bit more cheese and a sprinkling of basil, if using, and serve immediately.

$2.50 / SERVING
$5 TOTAL

Pasta with Eggplant and Tomato

This dish is similar to a traditional *pasta alla norma*, but without anchovies and ricotta salata. It's a perfect weeknight dinner in the summertime. I like to use a tubular pasta for this dish, but you can use anything, even spaghetti. The eggplant and tomatoes come together into a sauce that is thick, jammy, and savory.

SERVES 3, OR 2 VERY HUNGRY PEOPLE

salt

8 ounces rigatoni

2 tablespoons olive oil

1 large eggplant, cubed

4 cloves garlic, finely chopped

½ teaspoon chile flakes

2 cups finely diced canned tomatoes

¼ cup freshly grated Romano or Parmesan cheese

sprinkling of finely chopped fresh basil (optional)

pepper, to taste

1 Put a pot of water over high heat and add a good shake of salt. Bring it to a boil and cook the pasta according to the package instructions.

2 Meanwhile, set a wide pan over medium-high heat and splash in the olive oil. Let it get hot, then add the eggplant cubes, sprinkle with salt, and cook until the cubes start to brown, about 5 minutes. If the eggplant starts to look too dry, add a bit of water.

3 Once the cubes are a little brown on all sides, add the garlic and chile flakes and stir. Add the tomatoes and cook, stirring occasionally, about 15 minutes. Again, if it looks too dry, add a bit of water. Everything will shrink up and become a sort of loose, thick sauce.

4 Add half the cheese and half the basil, if using, and stir to combine.

5 Once the pasta is cooked, drain it and add it to the saucepan. Toss everything together, then turn off the heat. Add salt and pepper to taste, and serve in bowls sprinkled with the remaining Romano and basil.

Tomato and Tuna Spaghetti

We already know that a can of tuna can be great in a salad or sandwich for a quick, satisfying lunch, but those uses are just scratching the surface. Canned tuna has a light flavor and a lovely, flaky texture that goes well in all kinds of dishes where you'd like more protein. This traditional Italian pasta dish brings together common pantry items for a beautiful and quick weeknight dinner. SERVES 3, OR 2 VERY HUNGRY PEOPLE

salt, to taste

8 ounces spaghetti

1 tablespoon olive oil

4 cloves garlic, finely chopped

1 cup pureed or chopped canned tomatoes (see box, page 29)

1 can (5 ounces) tuna (see box)

½ cup grated Romano cheese

pepper, to taste

ADDITIONS

2 anchovy fillets, finely chopped

2 tablespoons chopped olives

¼ cup Breadcrumbs (page 158)

1 tablespoon capers

YOU CAN USE EITHER OIL- OR WATER-PACKED TUNA HERE. The oil-packed tuna will slip and slide over the noodles a little more easily, but the water-packed can work just fine if you add another tablespoon of olive oil along with it.

---

1 Boil a large pot of heavily salted water and cook the spaghetti according to the package instructions.

2 Meanwhile, make your sauce. Place a pan over medium heat and add the olive oil. Let it get warm, then add the garlic and sauté until it smells great, about 1 minute.

3 Add the pureed tomatoes to the garlic and swirl around the pan. Let the sauce warm up for 2 minutes before adding the tuna. Use a wooden spoon to break up the tuna, and cook until it's heated through, about 3 more minutes.

4 Add ¼ cup of the grated Romano, reserving the rest to sprinkle on top. Taste and add salt and pepper as needed. Turn down the heat as low as possible and place a lid over the pan to keep it warm while you finish boiling the spaghetti.

5 Once the spaghetti is ready, drain most of the water from the pot, reserving a small amount. Dump the spaghetti into the pan with the sauce and toss everything together. If the sauce isn't moving nicely and coating the noodles, add a little bit of the reserved pasta water and toss it some more.

6 Once the spaghetti is coated, serve it topped with the remaining Romano.

IF YOU WANT TO CREATE a more complex dish, include one or more of the additions. The anchovies, olives, and capers can be added to the sauce at the beginning, but use the breadcrumbs at the end with the reserved Romano for a little crunch.

Cauliflower Cheese

This is a classic side dish in Great Britain: creamy, cheesy sauce over cauliflower, baked in the oven until the edges get crunchy and bubbly. It's like a healthier and more flavorful version of macaroni and cheese. Try substituting broccoli or cooked winter squash for the cauliflower—everyone will love it. With broccoli, this dish becomes an interpretation of the classic sleazy broccoli with cheese sauce—but a little less sleazy. You can also add some breadcrumbs to the top of the dish before baking if you like extra crunch. Enjoy with a green salad. **SERVES 4**

2 teaspoons salt, plus more to taste

1 head cauliflower, cut into bite-size pieces

1 tablespoon butter, plus more for the baking dish

3 cloves garlic, finely chopped

½ teaspoon chile flakes

1 bay leaf

1 tablespoon all-purpose flour

1½ cups milk

6 ounces sharp Cheddar cheese, grated

pepper, to taste

ADDITIONS

1 tablespoon Dijon mustard

4 scallions, finely chopped

zest of 1 lemon

1 teaspoon smoked paprika

½ teaspoon dried thyme

Breadcrumbs (page 158)

sprinkling of finely chopped fresh basil

1 Preheat the oven to 400°F.

2 Bring a large pot of water to a boil over high heat. Add the salt and the cauliflower, then leave it for 4 minutes.

3 Meanwhile, butter a baking dish large enough to comfortably accommodate all the cauliflower. I usually use a pie dish. Drain the cauliflower and add it to the dish.

4 Melt the butter in a medium-size saucepan over medium heat. Add the garlic, chile flakes, and bay leaf and cook for about 1 minute. Add the flour and stir quickly. The flour-butter mixture is called a roux. You want the roux to get just a little brown—this will probably take another minute. Slowly add the milk to the pot, stirring all the while to incorporate the roux and make a creamy sauce.

5 Continue cooking the sauce, stirring occasionally, until it just comes to a boil, about 5 to 7 minutes. Once a couple of bubbles appear, turn off the heat and stir the cheese into the sauce. Include any additions at this point (except breadcrumbs). Taste the sauce and add salt and pepper as needed. Remove the bay leaf. The sauce should be creamy, smooth, and savory.

6 Pour the sauce over the cauliflower, sprinkling with breadcrumbs if desired. Place the dish in the oven and bake until the top is brown and bubbly, about 40 minutes.

Savory Summer Cobbler

Celebrate summer's most ubiquitous vegetables—tomatoes and zucchini—with a crunchy, peppery, Southern biscuit topping. For a variation, swap the zucchini for eggplant. Chop the eggplant into bite-size pieces, salt them, and set them aside for 30 minutes before using them in Step 2 as you would with the zucchini. SERVES 4

1 tablespoon olive oil, plus more for the pan

3 or 4 medium-size zucchini or summer squash, chopped into bite-size pieces

3 or 4 large tomatoes, canned or fresh, chopped into bite-size pieces (see box)

3 cloves garlic, finely chopped

4 scallions, finely chopped

zest of 1 lemon

¼ cup fresh basil (optional)

salt and pepper, to taste

TOPPING

½ cup (1 stick) unsalted butter

1½ cups all-purpose or whole-wheat flour

½ cup cornmeal

1 tablespoon baking powder

½ teaspoon salt

1 teaspoon black pepper

1 teaspoon smoked paprika

½ cup grated sharp Cheddar cheese, plus more for sprinkling

1 cup milk

sprinkling of fresh chopped herbs or scallions

1 Put the butter for the topping in the freezer for 30 minutes. Preheat the oven to 425°F.

2 Lightly oil an 8- by 10-inch baking dish (or any baking dish that will accommodate the vegetables) and pile in the zucchini, tomatoes, garlic, scallions, lemon zest, and basil, if using. Pour the olive oil over the top, scatter a generous amount of salt and pepper over everything, and mix it up with your hands. Bake the vegetables for 25 minutes while you prepare the biscuit topping.

3 Combine the flour, cornmeal, baking powder, salt, pepper, paprika, and cheese in a bowl.

4 Once the butter is frozen, use a box grater to flake it into the flour mixture. Gently massage the butter into the flour with your fingers until the mixture is crumbly but still clumpy. Add the milk and quickly bring the dough together. Don't knead it: Lumpiness is fine

and results in a flaky topping. Put it in the fridge until the vegetables come out of the oven.

5 Once the vegetable mixture has cooked for 25 minutes, remove it from the oven and quickly top it with small clumps of biscuit dough. The vegetables should still be visible in some areas.

6 Bake until the vegetables are bubbly and the topping is lightly browned, 20 to 25 minutes. Top with some more Cheddar and some chopped herbs or scallions.

IF YOU HAVE VERY LARGE AND JUICY TOMATOES, you might want to remove some of the seeds and juice so that the final dish is less watery. If a little juice doesn't bother you, just leave them as is.

Barley Risotto with Peas

Barley is sadly underused—other than in the odd soup, it rarely makes an appearance. What a shame! It has such a chewy, satisfying texture and nutty flavor. In this play on risotto, barley takes the place of Arborio rice for a dish that is less creamy, but more hearty and requires much less stirring. The pops of chewy barley and peas go well together, but as with regular risotto, you can use any vegetable—just adjust the cooking time depending on what you choose. For a more traditional risotto flavor, substitute Romano cheese for the ricotta. SERVES 3

1 cup pearl barley

5 cups broth (see box)

1 tablespoon butter

1 onion, chopped

3 cloves garlic, finely chopped

zest and juice of 1 lemon

2 cups frozen peas

½ cup Ricotta (page 163)

salt and pepper, to taste

2 slices bacon, chopped (optional—
     see box)

USE HOMEMADE BROTH IF POSSIBLE. I like vegetable, but chicken is fine. Beef or fish might be overwhelming, but could work if you use different vegetables. Even a bouillon cube dissolved in water is fine. Just don't buy boxed broth—it's a total rip-off.

1 Preheat the oven to 350°F.

2 Pour the barley onto a rimmed baking sheet, spreading it into an even layer. Place it in the oven and bake until the barley is golden brown, 10 minutes. If you're short on time, skip this step, but you'll lose out on the toasty flavor.

3 Place a small pot over low heat and add the broth. It just needs to heat up and stay warm.

4 Melt the butter in a large, heavy-bottomed pan over medium heat. Add the onion and cook until it becomes translucent, about 3 minutes. Add the garlic and cook for another minute.

5 Add the toasted barley and lemon zest, then stir to coat with the butter and onion. Add a ladleful (about ½ cup) of broth and stir. Cook for about 30 minutes, stirring occasionally and adding another ladleful of broth whenever the barley looks like it needs it. Reduce the heat if you notice the broth disappearing quickly.

6 At the 20-minute mark you should have used up about 4 cups of broth. Add the frozen peas and another ½ cup broth. Stir until the broth is absorbed. Try a piece of barley to see whether it is fully cooked. There should be no hard center and the barley should be soft, but still chewy and whole. If the barley is not quite cooked, add the remaining ½ cup broth, stir, and keep cooking. Once it's ready, add the lemon juice and ricotta and stir. Taste and add salt and pepper as needed. You should be generous with the pepper, but the salt will depend on the saltiness of your broth, so be mindful.

IF YOU WANT TO USE BACON, add it in Step 4 instead of the butter. Let the bacon get crispy and release its fat. Continue with Step 4.

Vegetable Jambalaya

I don't make jambalaya exactly the way they do down South, but this vegetable-heavy version is faster and just as good—a great, throw-everything-in-the-pot kind of meal. It's spicy, savory, and deeply satisfying. The leftovers are great for burritos or warmed up with a fried egg on top. SERVES 6

2 tablespoons vegetable oil or butter

1 medium-size onion, chopped

1 green bell pepper, stemmed, seeded, and chopped

3 stalks of celery, chopped

3 cloves garlic, finely chopped

½ small green chile, finely chopped

2 large tomatoes, chopped

2 bay leaves

1 teaspoon paprika

1 teaspoon garlic powder

1 teaspoon cayenne pepper

½ teaspoon dried thyme

½ teaspoon dried oregano

1 teaspoon Worcestershire sauce or soy sauce

¾ cup long-grain rice

3 cups vegetable or chicken broth

salt and pepper, to taste

ADDITIONS

slices of fried sausage

shrimp

leftover meat, tofu, or beans

1 Place a large, heavy-bottomed pot over medium-high heat and add the oil. After it gets hot, add the onion, bell pepper, and celery and cook for about 5 minutes, until they become translucent but not brown.

2 Add the garlic, chile, tomatoes, bay leaves, paprika, garlic powder, cayenne, thyme, oregano, salt, pepper, and Worcestershire sauce. Let everything cook until some of the tomato juice releases, about 1 minute.

3 Add the rice and slowly pour in the broth. Lower the heat to medium and let the dish cook until the rice absorbs all the liquid, 20 to 25 minutes. If you're using any of the additions, throw them in to cook with the rice after 15 minutes have passed.

4 Taste and adjust the salt, pepper, and any other spices.

Spicy, Crunchy, Creamy Polenta

Polenta + vegetable + egg = satisfying and delicious. You can also add a can of corn to the polenta for bursts of flavor. Or add frozen peas, scallions, olives, or (my favorite) green chiles to do something a little different. Or skip the Romano cheese and add ¼ cup of grated Cheddar for maximum cheese factor. SERVES 2

½ teaspoon salt, plus more to taste

½ cup polenta or cornmeal

4 cups fresh spinach or 1 cup thawed frozen spinach

3 cloves garlic

1 anchovy (optional)

1 tablespoon olive oil or butter

½ teaspoon chile flakes or 1 chopped fresh chile

2 eggs

sprinkling of freshly grated Romano or Parmesan cheese

pepper, to taste

1 Add 2 cups of water to a medium-size pot and bring it to a boil over medium-high heat. Add the salt, then turn the heat down to low and slowly pour in the polenta, stirring briskly with a wooden spoon. Stirring while pouring is crucial to make creamy, lump-free polenta. Once it's smooth and thick, leave the spoon in the pot and place a lid on it, slightly askew, so that steam can escape.

2 Let the polenta cook while you prepare the rest of the meal, checking in occasionally to give it a stir. The total cooking time should be 25 to 30 minutes, but if you're in a rush, you can eat it after 15.

3 Meanwhile, roughly chop the spinach. Finely chop the garlic and anchovy, if using, and set aside.

4 Place a pan over medium heat and add half the olive oil. Let the pan heat up until it sizzles when you flick it with water. Add the garlic, anchovy, and chile flakes. Let them cook until you can smell them, about 1 minute. Add the spinach and toss it around with tongs, or just swirl the pan to coat the spinach with the garlic mixture. Let everything cook until the spinach is wilted, 3 to 5 minutes. Turn off the heat and transfer the mixture to a bowl to wait for the polenta and eggs.

5 When the polenta is about 2 minutes from being done, start the eggs. Carefully wipe off the pan you just used, and put it back over medium heat. Add the remaining olive oil. When the oil is hot, crack the eggs into the pan and cover with a lid to steam them, 1 to 2 minutes. You'll have sunny-side-up eggs with fully cooked whites.

6 Scoop the polenta into two bowls. Add some Romano and lots of salt and pepper. Layer the spinach mixture over the polenta.

7 Once the whites have cooked, remove the eggs from the pan with a spatula and lay them over the spinach. Top with another sprinkling of cheese and a little more salt and pepper.

Tofu Hot Pot

I got really excited when my friend Iva asked for a recipe that featured the Chinese flavors she grew up with. After all, Chinese cooking depends on the same general principles as *Good and Cheap*: Build bright flavors from key ingredients, and use lots of veggies with just a little meat or fish. The ginger-garlic broth in this hot pot is spectacular! The effect of a small amount of toasted sesame oil is remarkable—an investment, but a transformative flavor. Use whatever vegetables you have around, but mushrooms help create an earthy broth.

SERVES 4

---

1 tablespoon finely grated ginger (see box)

4 cloves garlic, finely grated

½ pound mushrooms, chopped

1 teaspoon chile paste

2 tablespoons soy sauce

2 teaspoons toasted sesame oil

1 pound firm tofu

4 medium-size carrots, chopped

4 scallions, white and green parts, separated and chopped

8 ounces dried spaghetti, soba, or any Asian noodles

handful of bean sprouts (optional)

ADDITIONS

1 pound chicken, pork, or beef instead of tofu

handful of peanuts, chopped

cabbage

chile peppers, finely chopped

sprinkling of chopped fresh cilantro

kimchi, for topping

1 daikon radish, sliced, for topping

1 Place the grated ginger and garlic in a pot over medium heat. A few seconds later, once you start to smell the garlic, pour in 8 cups of water. Bring to a boil, then decrease the heat to low. Add the mushrooms, chile paste, soy sauce, and toasted sesame oil. Place a lid on the pot and let simmer for 20 minutes.

2 Cut the tofu into 4 slices, then cut each slice into 8 squares. (Or just chop it up however you like.)

3 Add the tofu, carrots, and the white parts of the scallions to the broth. Cook until the carrots are tender, about 10 minutes more.

4 Add the noodles and boil until they soften, usually just a few minutes, although it depends on the type of noodle. Check the package directions for specific cooking times.

5 Taste the broth. If it isn't salty enough, splash in more soy sauce. Adjust the sesame oil and chile paste to your taste as well.

6 Ladle the soup into bowls. For a little crunch, top with the bean sprouts, if using, and the green parts of the scallions.

> **WHEN YOU BUY GINGER,** just store it in the freezer. It's much easier to grate when frozen! You don't need to peel it—just grate and the skin will flake off. (It'll last for a couple of months.)

> **IF YOU HAVE LEFTOVERS,** you'll find you like this soup even more the next day. Overnight, the flavors will infuse into the tofu, as well as combining with each other. You might want to store the noodles separately, though, because otherwise they'll get mushy.

Deconstructed Cabbage Rolls

Casseroles are a great way to stretch your cooking-without-a-recipe muscles. As one reader, Carolie, reminded me, they require little prep time, yield many meals, and the leftovers will keep nicely in the fridge or freezer. So here's my adaptation of one of Carolie's favorite casseroles, itself a play on cabbage rolls, a traditional Eastern European dish that is delicious but labor-intensive. This version is a good way to use up leftover rice or grains and lentils, including leftover Rainbow Rice (page 164). For the sausage, I use fresh chorizo because it's easy to find in my neighborhood and I love the spicy, smoky flavor, but you should use whatever you like. SERVES 6

1 tablespoon butter

1 fresh sausage, about 4 ounces

1 onion, chopped

4 cloves garlic, finely chopped

1 small or ½ large cabbage, cored and chopped

salt and pepper, to taste

3 cups cooked rice (page 164)

4 cups cooked lentils

3½ cups pureed canned tomatoes or Best Tomato Sauce (page 127)

ADDITIONS

Breadcrumbs (page 158), for topping

olives

peas or corn

cheese

any spice combination (page 149)

VARIATIONS

ground beef, turkey, or pork instead of lentils and sausage

Swiss chard or collards instead of cabbage

1 Preheat the oven to 350°F. Lightly oil a large casserole dish.

2 Melt the butter in a large pan over medium heat. Slide the casing off the sausage and crumble the raw meat into the pan. Sauté the meat until it's no longer pink, about 5 minutes, then transfer to a large bowl.

3 Add the onion and garlic to the pan with the sausage drippings and sauté. Once the onion turns translucent, about 3 minutes, add the cabbage and sauté until it's tender enough to jab easily with a fork, 5 to 7 minutes. Season generously with salt and pepper.

4 While the cabbage cooks, mix the rice and lentils with the sausage in the bowl. Add salt, pepper, and any other spices or additions you'd like. Make sure you taste the mixture as you season it. If both parts of the casserole are tasty, you'll end up with a delicious meal. If they aren't seasoned well, it'll be bland.

5 Spread half of the lentil-rice-sausage mixture in an even layer in the casserole dish. Next, spread half of the cabbage mixture on top. Then, as evenly as possible, pour half of the pureed tomatoes over everything. Repeat the layers and sprinkle with salt and pepper. If adding breadcrumbs, sprinkle over the top.

6 Bake until the casserole is hot and bubbly, about 30 minutes.

method
ROASTED VEGETABLES

When the weather turns cool, I want to eat warm, flavorful food. Roasting is easy, it warms up the kitchen, and it makes the house smell like the holidays. If you're uncertain how to prepare a new vegetable, you usually can't go wrong with roasting—most things end up sweeter, with nice crunchy bits. If you roast a bunch of vegetables at the beginning of the week, you can eat them throughout the week in various ways: with eggs at breakfast, folded into an omelet, as a side dish, in a taco or sandwich, on toast, or with any grain.

olive oil or butter

salt and pepper, to taste

ROOTS

potatoes, sweet potatoes, beets, turnips, onions, parsnips, carrots, sunchokes, kohlrabi, fennel bulbs

NON-ROOTS

bell peppers, winter squash, broccoli, Brussels sprouts, cauliflower, asparagus, eggplant

ADDITIONS

whole, unpeeled garlic cloves

lemon slices or lemon zest

anything you would pair with roast chicken

tough herbs like sage, oregano, thyme, or bay leaves

any spice combination (page 149)

favorite sauce, a soft cheese, or mayonnaise, for serving

1 **Preheat the oven to 400°F.**

2 **Clean your vegetables.** Generally, I prefer to leave the skin on. Skin tastes nice and gets crispy, there's a lot of nutrition in the skin, and peeling is fussy! Just be sure to wash the vegetables thoroughly.

3 **Chop them up.** Many vegetables are nice roasted whole, like new potatoes or little sunchokes or turnips—they will be crispy and salty on the outside and bursting with fluffy, starchy goodness inside. However, the general rule is that the smaller you chop things, the faster they cook, so try to keep everything about the same size.

4 Dump your vegetables into a roasting pan. Drizzle everything with olive oil or melted butter—about 2 tablespoons per standard-size roasting pan. Season generously with salt and pepper and add any other additions from the list. Use your hands to coat the vegetables thoroughly with the oil and spices.

5 Pop the pan in the oven. Root vegetables generally need to bake for at least 1 hour or longer, but check on them after 30 minutes. Non-roots need only 25 to 30 minutes, so check on those earlier. Poke them with a knife to test their doneness. If the knife meets no resistance, they're finished; if not, let them cook longer (you don't want undercooked root vegetables in particular—they're awful). Don't worry about leaving them in too long. Unlike vegetables overcooked through boiling or steaming, overcooked roasted vegetables may dry out a bit, but they still retain their shape and flavor.

6 After you pull the vegetables out of the oven, **push them around with a spatula to free them from the pan.** Remove any garlic cloves and smash them into a fine paste (remove the skins at this point), then put the garlic back in the pan and mix together. Squeeze the juice out of any lemons and discard the woody bits of any cooked herbs.

7 Add a little more butter, a bit of a favorite sauce, or a little soft cheese or mayonnaise, and serve.

Chana Masala

This Indian chickpea dish is a beloved staple in my home. If you don't have cooked chickpeas, you can use canned, but it will cost about $1 more. For a full meal, serve the chana masala over rice or with Roti (page 152). SERVES 2

1 tablespoon ground coriander

1 teaspoon ground turmeric

¼ teaspoon cayenne powder

½ teaspoon garam masala

1 teaspoon smoked paprika
   (optional)

½ teaspoon salt, plus more to taste

½ tablespoon ghee (see box)
   or ½ tablespoon butter plus a
   splash of olive oil

1 teaspoon cumin seeds

1 small onion, chopped

3 cloves garlic, finely chopped

1 teaspoon grated ginger

½ jalapeño pepper, finely chopped
   (remove seeds for less heat)

1 cup pureed canned tomatoes
   (see box, page 29)

2½ cups cooked chickpeas, drained

GARNISHES
chopped fresh cilantro

Raita (page 147) or yogurt

1 Combine the coriander, turmeric, cayenne, garam masala, smoked paprika, if using, and salt in a small bowl.

2 Melt the ghee in a small saucepan over medium-low heat. Once it begins to sizzle, add the cumin seeds and stir for about 5 seconds until you can smell them. Add the onion and sauté until it's a little soft, 2 to 3 minutes. Add the garlic and cook for 2 minutes. Add the ginger and jalapeño and cook for 1 minute longer. Add the spice mixture you made in Step 1, then the pureed tomatoes. Mix, then put a lid on the pan and let everything cook down, 5 to 10 minutes.

3 Once the tomato has reduced and the ghee starts to separate from the sauce, add the chickpeas and ½ cup of water. Stir, bring it to a boil, and then decrease the heat to a simmer. Cook for 10 minutes, and then squish a few chickpeas with the back of a spoon to thicken the sauce before serving. Garnish with cilantro and Raita (page 147).

GHEE, a traditional staple in Indian cooking, is just butter with the milk solids removed. It can withstand higher temperatures than butter without burning. You can make it at home by melting butter and letting the white milk solids rise to the top. Scoop them out and discard them. The leftover golden liquid is ghee. Store it in the fridge.

Black-Eyed Peas and Collards

This is similar to the Southern classic Hoppin' John, but streamlined into a one-pot meal, where you cook the collards with the beans instead of on their own. If you have them, you can add more vegetables to the base along with the onion—celery, carrot, bell pepper, and some canned tomatoes would all be great in this. If you want to skip the bacon, just add smoked paprika to replace the smoky flavor. This dish pairs well with rice, any other grain, or with some toast or flatbread. **SERVES 4**

1 cup dried black-eyed peas

1 tablespoon butter

1 large onion, finely chopped

3 cloves garlic, finely chopped

3 strips bacon, cut into small pieces

1 bay leaf

1 large bunch collard greens

1 teaspoon salt, plus more to taste

pepper, to taste

1 Place the black-eyed peas and 4 cups of water in a bowl and soak overnight.

2 Melt the butter in a large saucepan over medium heat. Add the onion, garlic, bacon, and bay leaf. Cover the pan with a lid and leave it for 2 minutes. Stir occasionally and cook until the onion is translucent and the bacon is starting to crisp, about 5 minutes.

3 Drain the black-eyed peas and pour them into the saucepan. Cover them with water and turn the heat down to medium-low. Cook for 30 minutes to 2 hours. The cooking time will depend on how old the peas are, which is difficult to predict. The peas are done when you can easily squish them on the countertop with the back of a spoon. Check on them every half hour or so, and if water boils off, add more water (hot, preferably) to cover them.

4 While the peas cook, line up several leaves of collard greens on a cutting board and slice the tough central stem away from the leaves. Discard the stems. Thoroughly wash the collards and chop them into bite-size pieces. Alternatively, use your hands to tear the collards into small pieces.

5 Once the peas are cooked, add the collards to the pot and put the lid back on. Add the salt and some freshly ground pepper, then stir. Taste the liquid and peas and add more salt as needed. Cover the pan with a lid and leave until the collards are tender, 10 to 15 minutes. Remove from the heat and serve.

Vegetable Quiche, Hold the Crust

As much as I love this quiche hot, I like it even better cold out of the fridge the next day. It makes a great fast breakfast or lunch (paired with a side salad). The quiche in the picture uses broccoli, but you can make it with pretty much any kind of vegetable. Some of my favorites are roasted green chiles and Cheddar, winter squash with goat cheese, zucchini and tomato, or spinach and olive. Spreading out onions on the bottom of the quiche adds a crust-like layer and a bit of crunch. SERVES 4

1 tablespoon butter

1 large onion, sliced into half-moons

1 teaspoon salt, plus more to taste

½ teaspoon pepper, plus more to taste

3 to 4 cups chopped vegetables (see box)

8 eggs

1 cup milk

1 cup grated Cheddar or other cheese

1 Preheat the oven to 400°F.

2 Melt the butter in a cast-iron or ovenproof skillet over medium heat. (If your skillet isn't ovenproof, transfer everything to a pie plate in Step 3 to bake it.) Add the onion slices and sprinkle a bit of salt and pepper over them. Cook the onions until they are golden brown and starting to caramelize, about 10 minutes.

3 Remove the pan from the heat and spread the onions evenly across the bottom. Spread the vegetables evenly over the onions. The dish or pan should look fairly full.

4 In a bowl, use a fork to beat the eggs lightly with the milk, cheese, 1 teaspoon of salt, and ½ teaspoon of pepper, just enough to break up the yolks and whites. This is a savory custard mixture. Pour the custard over the vegetables and onions and enjoy watching it fill in all the open spaces.

5 Transfer the quiche to the oven and bake for 1 hour. Once the surface is lightly brown all the way across, it's fully cooked.

6 Let the quiche cool for about 20 minutes, then slice into wedges.

FOR HARDIER VEGETABLES LIKE BROCCOLI, cauliflower, or winter squash, I suggest steaming or cooking them before adding them to the quiche to ensure they'll be fully cooked. For tomatoes, zucchini, spinach, or any other quick-cooking vegetable, just use them fresh.

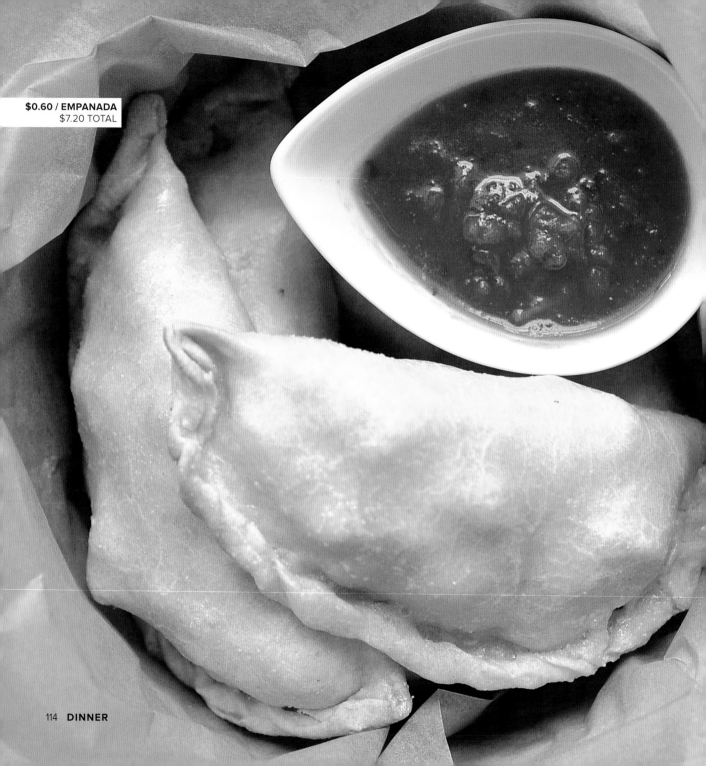

$0.60 / EMPANADA
$7.20 TOTAL

Broccoli, Egg, and Cheddar Empanadas

Every culture has some version of dough stuffed with tasty filling—it's a perfect combination. So empanadas, dumplings, pierogi, and calzones in one book isn't that crazy—right? My friend Barb felt the same way, so I created this recipe for her. The cornmeal isn't traditional in empanadas—I just like the extra crunch it gives. You can substitute more flour for the cornmeal if you like. MAKES 12 EMPANADAS

oil or butter, for the baking sheet

DOUGH

¼ cup (½ stick) butter

2 cups all-purpose or whole-wheat flour, plus more for rolling the dough

½ cup cornmeal

½ teaspoon salt

1 egg

½ cup cold water

FILLING

4 cups chopped broccoli, florets and stems

8 eggs

2 cloves garlic, finely chopped

½ teaspoon chile flakes

salt and pepper, to taste

1 cup grated sharp Cheddar cheese

IF YOU OWN A PASTRY BRUSH, an egg wash will make the empanadas shinier. Since it only affects appearance, this step is optional. To make the egg wash, beat an egg with a fork in a small bowl, then brush the tops of the empanadas.

---

1 Preheat the oven to 400°F. Lightly oil or butter 2 baking sheets.

2 Make the dough: Place the ¼ cup butter in the freezer for 10 minutes. Meanwhile, mix the flour, cornmeal, and salt in a large bowl. Grate the cold butter directly into the flour mixture. Use clean hands to squish the butter gently into the flour until it looks like breadcrumbs.

3 Make a crater in the flour mixture. Crack 1 egg into it and pour in the cold water. Mix with your hands until the dough comes together into a smooth ball. If you're using whole-wheat flour and the dough seems dry, add another tablespoon of water. Wrap the ball of dough in plastic or cover it with a moist towel.

4 Make the filling: Place a large pan over medium heat and add the broccoli and 1 cup water. Cover it with a lid and cook until the water is gone and the broccoli is tender, 5 to 7 minutes.

5 Meanwhile, crack the 8 eggs into a bowl. Add the garlic, chile flakes, salt, and pepper, and beat lightly to combine.

6 Once the broccoli is tender, pour the eggs into the pan with the broccoli and stir until the eggs are just scrambled, about 2 minutes. Turn off the heat, add the cheese, and stir again.

7 Dust a clean countertop lightly with flour. Unwrap the dough and divide it into 12 equal pieces. Roll each piece into a ball with your hands, then use a rolling pin to flatten each ball into a thin circle, a little bigger than a coaster. Place some filling—about a heaping ⅓ cup—on one side of the circle, then fold over the other side to form a half-moon. Pinch the edges together and place the empanada on the prepared baking sheet. Repeat!

8 Bake until the empanadas turn golden brown, about 20 minutes. Cool for 10 minutes before serving.

Potato and Kale Rolls with Raita

These are a great meal to make when you have leftover Roti (page 152) and Raita (page 147). The possibilities for fillings are endless—this quick version with potatoes and greens is tasty and satisfying. **SERVES 4**

1 tablespoon ghee or butter (see box, page 109)

1 teaspoon cumin seeds

1 small onion, finely chopped

3 cloves garlic, finely chopped

1 tablespoon finely grated ginger

1 teaspoon ground turmeric

1 teaspoon ground coriander

1 teaspoon cayenne pepper

1 teaspoon salt, plus more to taste

2 large or 4 medium-size potatoes, chopped

1 bunch kale or spinach, stems removed, chopped

8 Roti (half the recipe on page 152)

sprinkling of chopped fresh cilantro

Raita (page 147)

1 Place a skillet over medium heat and add the ghee. Once it is hot, add the cumin seeds and let them sizzle for 5 seconds before adding the onion. Let the onion cook for 2 minutes, stirring occasionally.

2 In a small bowl, combine the garlic, ginger, turmeric, coriander, cayenne pepper, salt, and 1 tablespoon water.

3 Add the spices to the onion mixture and cook, stirring, for another 2 minutes. It will smell strongly aromatic. This step is important because the spices will toast and release their flavor.

4 Next, add the potatoes and stir them with the onion and spice mixture to coat. Add about a cup of water and cover the pan with a lid. Let the potatoes cook until tender, about 10 minutes, stirring occasionally. Add more water as needed. The water helps everything cook evenly, but you want the final mixture to be dry potatoes with just enough moisture to keep them from sticking. When you add water, be sure to let it cook off.

5 Test the potatoes with a fork: If you can easily pierce them, they're ready. Once they are, add the kale and stir until the kale is wilted, 1 to 2 minutes. Taste and add more salt if needed.

6 To assemble the rolls, scoop ⅛ of the mixture into the center of a roti, distributing it in an even line. Roll it up.

7 Serve 2 roti per person with cilantro and a generous dollop of raita, either inside the wrap or on the side.

ideas
STUFF ON HOT DOGS

Although you might eat hot dogs with great delight on a sunny day, they don't feel so exciting when they're all you have in the fridge, or all a picky child will eat. But don't get stuck thinking hot dogs are boring. Whether pork, beef, kosher, or veggie, hot dogs are livelier with a generous vegetable topping. Here are some ideas to get you going.

❶ Quick Teriyaki Carrots
$0.75 TOTAL

This quick teriyaki sauce is great on all kinds of vegetables. Try it with carrots and then experiment from there.

2 tablespoons soy sauce
1 teaspoon brown sugar
1 clove garlic, grated
2 to 3 carrots, grated

1 Add the soy sauce, brown sugar, and garlic to a hot pan over medium heat. Let it sizzle.

2 Once the sugar is dissolved, toss the carrots in and cook until they absorb the sauce, about 2 minutes.

❷ Salt and Vinegar Cucumbers with Dill
$1.20 TOTAL

These tangy cucumbers are like a quick form of pickles. Add a tablespoon of dill or mustard seeds for a more pickley flavor. Store leftovers in a sealed container in the fridge and they'll keep about a week.

1 field cucumber
2 tablespoons vinegar
1 teaspoon salt

1 Thinly slice the cucumber.

2 Scoop the cucumber into a bowl with the vinegar and salt and toss. Marinate for 20 minutes.

❸ Mexican Street Corn
(page 47)

Simply cut the corn off the cob and mix the mayo, chili powder, cheese, and lime into the kernels.

❺ Wilted Cabbage Salad
(page 43)

Chop the cabbage finely so that it can be distributed evenly over your hot dog.

❹ Salsa (page 145)

Try to drain a little bit of the juice so it doesn't make your bun too soggy. Crumble tortilla chips on top for some crunch.

❻ Sweet or Savory Pineapple Salad
(page 30)

This is a classic combo, especially with pork! Chop the pineapple finely so it won't fall off.

Potato Leek Pizzas

Obviously you should just make all kinds of pizza. Seriously, do it. Make it a Thursday-night tradition and an excuse to use up leftovers. This pizza is a fun variation that confounds expectations—proof that, indeed, anything is good on pizza! **MAKES 4 PERSONAL PIZZAS**

---

2 tablespoons olive oil

1 large russet potato or 3 small potatoes, sliced into thin circles

salt and pepper, to taste

3 leeks, trimmed, washed, and sliced into circles

all-purpose flour, for shaping the dough

1 recipe Pizza Dough (page 156)

1 pound fresh mozzarella cheese, shredded

1 Preheat the oven to 500°F.

2 Place a large pan over medium heat and add 1 tablespoon of the olive oil. Once the oil is hot, add as many potato slices as will fit in the pan, spacing them out to make sure each slice is touching the bottom. (If you slice them thinly enough, they'll turn out almost like little chips.)

3 Let the potatoes cook until they start to crinkle around the edges and turn brown, about 2 minutes. Flip them over and brown the other side, another minute or so, then move them to a bowl. Continue in batches, as needed. Sprinkle with salt and pepper, then (after they cool down!) toss with your hands to make sure they're evenly coated.

4 Heat the remaining tablespoon of oil in the same pan, then throw in the leeks, stirring occasionally until they're soft, about 5 minutes. Toss them in the bowl with the potato slices, add a bit more salt and pepper, and stir.

5 Sprinkle flour on a clean countertop. Divide the pizza dough into 4 equal pieces and place one piece on the countertop. Using your hands or a rolling pin, stretch the dough into crust. I like to make mine really thin and big, but it's up to you how thick to make it.

6 Once the crust is the desired shape and thickness, dust the back of a baking sheet with flour to keep the crust from sticking, then place the crust on the sheet.

7 Layer a quarter of the potato and leek mixture on top of the crust and sprinkle with a quarter of the shredded mozzarella. Bake for 5 to 8 minutes. If it's your first time, simply keep an eye on the oven to see when the pizza's done. The crust should be light brown and the cheese melted. Repeat the process until you've baked all your pizzas. If your oven is big enough, you can, of course, do more than one pizza at a time.

Broccoli Rabe and Mozzarella Calzones

Calzones are pizza in a slightly different form—a form that lets you stuff in more filling without weighing down the crust. Broccoli rabe is great, but you can use any bitter green, or even broccoli or cauliflower. You'll love these crusty pockets full of oozy goodness! **MAKES 4 CALZONES**

all-purpose flour or cornmeal, for shaping the dough

1 tablespoon olive oil

1 large bunch broccoli rabe, chopped

4 cloves garlic, finely chopped

1 teaspoon chile flakes

2 anchovy fillets, finely chopped (optional)

salt and pepper, to taste

1 recipe Pizza Dough (page 156)

2 cups grated mozzarella cheese

IF YOU HAVE ITALIAN SAUSAGE in your fridge, crumble it into the pan with the broccoli rabe in Step 2. Sausage and broccoli rabe are a classic combination.

1 Preheat the oven to 500°F (or as hot as your oven gets). Sprinkle a small amount of flour over a baking sheet and set it aside.

2 Place a large pan over medium heat and add the olive oil. Once the oil is hot, add the tough stem ends of the broccoli rabe and cook for 2 minutes. Next, add the rest of the broccoli rabe, including the leafy parts, along with the garlic, chile flakes, and the anchovies, if using. Cook, stirring occasionally, until the stems are tender, about 5 minutes. Add salt and pepper, and set the filling aside.

3 Sprinkle flour on a clean countertop. Divide the pizza dough into 4 equal pieces and place one piece on the countertop. Using your hands or a rolling pin, roll out the dough as you would for pizza (page 120), until it is quite thin.

4 Pile a quarter of the broccoli rabe mixture and ½ cup of the mozzarella onto one side of the circle, leaving a lip around the edge.

5 Gather up the half of the dough that isn't weighed down with filling and fold it over to create a half-moon shape. Pinch the edges of the dough together. Place the calzone carefully on the prepared baking sheet and repeat Steps 3 to 5 until you have 4 calzones.

6 Bake until the calzones are golden brown on the outside, 6 to 8 minutes. Be careful when you bite into them—they'll be hot!

Half-Veggie Burgers

When a reader named Quinn suggested a recipe that used both lentils and meat, I started thinking about how veggie burgers and beef burgers each have their own strengths. Why not combine the two ideas to create a burger with meaty flavor but the lean protein and low cost of lentils? And so I offer you the half-veggie burger. May it rest a little lighter in your belly.

You can use almost any vegetable to make these burger patties, except for lettuce and other greens, or super-watery vegetables like tomato or cucumber. Make sure the vegetables are either small to begin with (like corn or peas) or finely chopped so that they cook evenly. I went for a bell pepper this time. Vegetables like potato, squash, or eggplant, which are inedible raw, should be fully cooked before you add them to the patty. SERVES 8

3 cups cooked lentils or beans

1 cup finely chopped bell pepper or other vegetable

1 pound ground beef or other ground meat

1 egg (optional)

salt and pepper, to taste

8 buns

1 Roughly mash the lentils with the back of a large spoon.

2 Mix the lentils, bell pepper, and ground beef with your hands in a large bowl. If you're grilling, add an egg to keep the patties from crumbling. Season with salt and pepper and form into 8 patties.

3 Place a large skillet over medium-high heat (or fire up the grill, if you have one), and add the patties. Sear them until they're dark brown on one side, about 5 minutes, then flip 'em and do the same on the other side. If you want cheeseburgers, lay cheese on the patties after flipping them once.

4 Serve on toasted buns with your favorite condiments and fresh vegetables. Burgers are a great place to be adventurous!

IF YOU WON'T EAT all of the burgers at once, wrap any leftover raw patties in plastic. They will keep in the refrigerator for a few days or in the freezer for up to 2 weeks.

BIG BATCH

Best Tomato Sauce

There are many ways to make tomato sauce. I don't find that the more complex recipes taste any better—this one is boldly tomatoey and works on just about anything. It also takes 5 minutes to make. Can't beat that. MAKES 7 CUPS

2 tablespoons olive oil
6 cloves garlic, finely chopped
1 teaspoon chile flakes
2 cans (28 ounces each) tomatoes, crushed or diced
zest of 1 lemon (optional)
salt and pepper, to taste

1 Add the olive oil to a saucepan over medium heat.

2 Sauté the garlic until it smells great and becomes translucent, 1 minute. Add the chile flakes and cook for 30 seconds.

3 Add the cans of tomatoes, mix, and cook until warmed through.

4 Add the lemon zest, if using, then salt and pepper to taste. Because canned tomatoes are often already salted, you may not need to add any.

> **IF YOU WANT A THICKER SAUCE** that will stick to pasta better, cook it a little longer to evaporate more of the liquid, 10 to 20 minutes. Use immediately, keep in a jar in the fridge for up to a week, or portion it out into containers and store in the freezer for a month.

Chorizo and White Bean Ragù

After my friend Chris told me he loves a good ragù, I developed a version that is as hearty as a meaty tomato sauce without the cost and heaviness of a traditional ragù. A batch of this is probably enough for eight people, served with grated Romano or Parmesan cheese over pasta (page 160), polenta (page 100), or grits. **MAKES 6 CUPS**

2 tablespoons butter or vegetable oil

2 onions, chopped

6 cloves garlic, finely chopped

2 tablespoons finely chopped jalapeño (optional)

1 pound fresh chorizo, casing removed (or other fresh sausage)

3 cups canned or fresh tomatoes, pureed

3 cups cooked cannellini, navy, or butter beans

salt and pepper, to taste

1 Melt the butter in a pan over medium heat, swirling it to coat the pan. Add the chopped onions and cook until they turn translucent, 3 to 4 minutes.

2 Toss in the garlic, jalapeño (if using), and fresh chorizo, then sauté for about a minute. Add the tomatoes and beans, then simmer until the sauce is thick and the sausage is cooked, about 5 minutes. Taste and add salt and pepper as needed.

> **FREEZE THIS SAUCE** if you don't intend to eat it within a few days. It won't keep very long in the fridge.

Dark and Spicy Chili

Chili is such a crowd-pleaser. If you don't already have your own award-winning recipe, give this one a try.
To stretch this recipe even further, serve it with rice. SERVES 12

2 tablespoons ground cumin

2 tablespoons dried oregano

2 tablespoons ground coriander

1 tablespoon ground cinnamon

2 tablespoons cocoa powder

1 to 4 canned chipotle chiles in adobo, finely chopped

1 pound ground beef or turkey

1 pound Mexican chorizo (fresh, casings removed), or 1 pound more ground beef or turkey

2 medium-size onions, chopped

6 cloves garlic, finely chopped

2 bell peppers, stemmed, seeded, and chopped

2 carrots, chopped

6 cups cooked black beans

2 cans (28 ounces each) diced or crushed tomatoes

1 tablespoon salt, plus more to taste

TO SERVE

chopped scallions

chopped fresh cilantro

sour cream

cheddar cheese

1 In a small bowl, combine the cumin, oregano, coriander, cinnamon, cocoa powder, and chiles, and stir well. If it's your first time making this chili, use one or two chipotles. You can always add more, but you can't take away!

2 Place a large pot over medium heat and add the ground beef and chorizo. Cook the meat, breaking it up and stirring, until it is no longer pink. The fat from the meat should be enough to keep everything from sticking to the pot.

3 Add the spice mixture to the meat and stir until you can smell the spices, about 20 seconds. Add the onions, garlic, peppers, and carrots, and stir. Place a lid on the pot and cook, stirring occasionally, until the onion is translucent, about 10 minutes.

4 Add the black beans, tomatoes, and 4 cups of water, then stir. Bring the mixture to a boil, then turn the heat to low and simmer for 1½ hours with the lid askew to allow steam to escape. Taste and season with salt and pepper.

5 Serve in big bowls topped with scallions and cilantro, if using, or freeze in small portions for later.

TO MAKE VEGETARIAN CHILI, use a bit of oil to brown the onions and substitute more beans and veggies for the meat. Most of the flavor comes from the spices and vegetables, so you won't miss much.

YOU CAN USE ½ cup chili powder instead of the cumin, oregano, coriander, and chipotles in the spice mixture—just add the cinnamon and cocoa for a hint of sweetness.

TO MAKE IN A SLOW COOKER, follow the instructions up to Step 3, then transfer the mixture to the slow cooker, and add the rest of the ingredients. Cook on low for 8 to 10 hours.

Spicy Pulled Pork

Pulled pork is incredibly flavorful, rich, spicy, and remarkably versatile. Although it seems expensive, it's quite a bargain when you look at the price per serving. As with many special meals, this one takes quite a long time to prepare. Most of the time, however, is just spent waiting for it to cook "low and slow."

My favorite way to serve pulled pork is over squishy hamburger buns or in tacos with crunchy vegetables. Pulled pork sandwiches are great with cabbage slaw, so try using the Wilted Cabbage Salad (page 43). Serve with a simple green salad, corn on the cob, steamed green beans, or any other summery vegetables. SERVES 10

⅓ cup brown sugar

2 tablespoons ground coffee

2 tablespoons kosher salt

4 teaspoons smoked paprika

3 teaspoons sweet paprika

2 teaspoons ground cumin

1 teaspoon ground coriander

1 teaspoon ground cloves

1 teaspoon garlic powder

1 teaspoon black pepper

1 pork shoulder (about 5 pounds)

1 Make a dry rub by mixing all of the ingredients except the pork in a small bowl.

2 Apply the rub liberally to the pork shoulder, pressing it gently into the meat until you've covered every side. Set any leftover rub aside for later.

3 Place the pork shoulder in a large pot with a tight-fitting lid. Leave it in the fridge for 2 hours or overnight to let the flavors seep in.

4 Preheat the oven to 200°F.

5 Pour enough water into the pot to cover the bottom. Put the lid on and place the pot in the oven for 10 to 12 hours. The rule of thumb is 1½ to 2 hours per pound of pork, but I find it usually takes a little longer than that. You want the internal temperature to reach 200°F.

If you don't have a meat thermometer, figuring out the internal temperature is trickier, but you can test it by feel. Poke the meat with a finger: When it's so soft that it falls apart on its own, take it out of the oven. It's hard to overcook it at such a low temperature, so don't be too concerned about that.

6 Remove the meat from the juices and gently tear the pork apart with two forks or your hands. Discard any larger bits of fat. If any section is hard to tear apart, the meat hasn't cooked enough. If you have the time to spare, put it back in the oven for another couple of hours.

7 Once you've pulled all of the pork, mix in any remaining rub and transfer it to a casserole dish or a large plate. If you aren't eating the meat right away, stash it in the fridge, covered, for 3 to 4 days.

TO MAKE A SAUCE from the pot full of drippings, bring them to a gentle boil in a pot over medium-high heat and let the juices thicken for 20 to 30 minutes. The fat will rise to the top: It's the clear, thick layer, not the thin, red liquid below. Skim off as much of the fat as possible. Mix a few spoonfuls of the pan drippings with the pork before serving.

ideas
HUMMUS

Hummus is my go-to snack when hunger hits midafternoon. I often double or triple this recipe and freeze it. A food processor makes things easier, but without one all is not lost. After all, hummus was invented long before food processors.

IF YOU HAVE dried chickpeas, cook them using the instructions on page 165. Canned chickpeas will increase the cost of the recipes. (I also think the flavor of dried beans is better.)

UNLESS YOU ARE extremely thorough and patient with your handmade hummus, you will have a chunkier texture than the super-smooth and creamy store-bought hummus. It will still taste great, though!

Basic Hummus

SERVES 4

2 cups cooked chickpeas (see box)
1 tablespoon tahini
1 tablespoon lemon juice
1 clove garlic, finely chopped
1 tablespoon olive oil, plus more for serving
salt and pepper, to taste

1 *If you are making the hummus by hand*, warm the chickpeas for about 30 seconds in the microwave.

2 Mash the tahini, lemon juice, garlic, olive oil, salt, and pepper in a bowl.

3 Slowly add ¼ cup water a bit at a time, mashing as you add it, until the mixture is smooth, creamy, and light, about 5 minutes. Taste it and adjust the seasoning. Add more oil and tahini if you want it richer.

1 *If you are using a food processor*, add all the ingredients to the processor along with ⅛ cup water.

2 Once the mixture is a smooth paste, taste it to check the consistency. For a smoother and lighter hummus, add a bit more water. Taste it and adjust the seasoning. Add more oil and tahini if you want it richer.

❶ Roasted Garlic
$0.50 SERVING / $2 TOTAL

1 Preheat the oven to 350°F.

2 Slice the top off of a head of garlic so that you can see the cloves (leave the peel). Drizzle the cloves with olive oil. Wrap in tinfoil and place on a tray in the oven. Roast for 1 hour.

3 Remove the garlic from the oven. When it is cool enough to touch, gently squeeze all but 3 of the garlic cloves into the hummus and mix according to the basic recipe.

4 Finely chop the leftover garlic cloves and sprinkle on top of the hummus with extra olive oil.

❷ Lemon
$0.45 SERVING / $1.80 TOTAL

Replace the ¼ cup water with 3 tablespoons lemon juice and 1 tablespoon water. Add the zest of 1 lemon.

❸ Chipotle
$0.45 SERVING / $1.80 TOTAL

Add 1 or 2 chipotles in adobo to the hummus. If you're not using a food processor, make sure the chipotle is finely chopped. Mix a bit of adobo sauce with olive oil and drizzle over the top.

ideas
DEVILED EGGS

Deviled eggs are my favorite party food and the perfect recipe to dedicate to my friend Camilla. At parties, I often eat too much random junk food and end up feeling gross. These eggs are a great antidote: festive and delicious without the empty calories. Although they're a little fussy, they aren't actually difficult to make. Here's the formula: Make a basic deviled egg and add one of the 8 flavors (or create your own!).

12 eggs
salt and pepper, to taste
2 scallions, finely chopped
   (optional)
dash of paprika (optional)

HARD-BOILED EGGS ARE EASIER TO PEEL if the eggs you boil aren't quite fresh, so try making these with eggs that have been sitting in the fridge a week or two.

$0.15 / HALF EGG
$3.60 TOTAL

Basic Deviled Eggs

MAKES 24 HALF EGGS

1 Place a layer of eggs at the bottom of a pot that is large enough to fit them all with a bit of wiggle room. If you can't fit all your eggs, don't stack them—they might crack. Hard-boil them in batches instead.

2 Cover the eggs with cold water. Place the pot over medium heat and bring to a boil. As soon as the water is boiling, turn off the heat and cover the pot with a tight-fitting lid. Set a timer for 10 minutes.

3 When the timer goes off, carefully pour out the hot water and cover the eggs with very cold water. The cold water stops the cooking process so that you don't end up with that slightly icky blue-green skin around your yolk.

4 Peel the eggs. Everyone has his or her own technique, but I like to gently roll each egg across the counter to crack the shell. Roll the egg around until it looks like a cracked desert landscape, then peel it starting from the bottom (where the air pocket is). Once peeled, rinse the egg and set it aside. Repeat until you have peeled all the eggs.

5 Slice each egg in half lengthwise. Pop the yolks out and put them in a medium-size bowl. Don't worry if you leave a little yolk behind. Set the whites aside on a plate.

6 Sprinkle the yolks with salt and pepper, then add the other ingredients of your choice to the bowl. Mash with a fork until you have a relatively smooth paste.

7 Spoon the yolk mixture back into each egg. Pile the filling high! Alternatively, scoop the filling into a plastic sandwich bag. Cut off the corner of the sandwich bag and squeeze the yolk mixture into the whites.

8 Sprinkle with the scallions and some paprika for color, if you have it.

1 Classic

2 tablespoons mustard

2 tablespoons mayonnaise

2 tablespoons water, pickle brine, or lemon juice

2 Chile and Lime

2 tablespoons mayonnaise

2 tablespoons lime juice

1 jalapeño pepper, finely chopped (remove seeds for less heat)

3 Ramen-Inspired

2 tablespoons mayonnaise

2 tablespoons soy sauce

1 tablespoon rice vinegar

chili sauce, to taste

4 Curried

2 tablespoons mayonnaise

2 tablespoons water

4 teaspoons curry powder, or 1 teaspoon each of turmeric, cayenne, coriander, and cumin

5 Tomato

2 tablespoons mayonnaise

¼ cup finely chopped fresh or canned tomatoes or Best Tomato Sauce (page 127)

6 Chile and Cheese

2 tablespoons mayonnaise

2 tablespoons chopped green chiles

2 tablespoons grated cheese

7 Chorizo

2 tablespoons mayonnaise

2 tablespoons cooked, minced fresh chorizo

1 teaspoon paprika

8 Feta and Dill

2 tablespoons mayonnaise

2 tablespoons crumbled feta

1 tablespoon chopped dill

Pierogi

This recipe is huge and will feed you for days. It takes time and effort, but the results are worth it. The best approach is to invite a couple of friends over for a pierogi-making party. Everyone takes home a bag or two for the freezer, and it's a great time! For the filling, you should play around with some of your favorite things—there aren't many flavors that don't work in potatoes. I usually use several additions and a strong, aged cheddar. **MAKES 60 TO 72 PIEROGI**

DOUGH

4½ cups all-purpose flour, plus more for shaping the dough

2 teaspoons salt

2 cups yogurt or sour cream

2 eggs

FILLING

5 russet potatoes, roughly cubed

salt and pepper, to taste

1½ cups shredded sharp Cheddar cheese

ADDITIONS

2 scallions, chopped

4 cloves roasted garlic (page 135)

2 tablespoons Dijon mustard

1 teaspoon cayenne pepper

1 teaspoon paprika

TO SERVE

1 tablespoon butter

scallions, chopped

sour cream

1 In a large bowl, mix the flour and salt. Pour in the yogurt, eggs, and 1 tablespoon of water. Mix everything slowly and carefully with clean hands until it comes together into a smooth dough. The dough will be quite sticky. Cover it with a towel or plastic wrap while you make the filling.

2 Put the chopped potatoes in a pot. Cover with water, then add a bit of salt. Cover with a lid and bring to a boil over medium-high heat. Remove the lid and cook the potatoes until tender, about 20 minutes. Test them with a fork. If it goes through easily, they're done.

3 Drain the potatoes and add the shredded cheese, salt, pepper, and any additions you might enjoy.

4 Mash the potatoes with an electric mixer or two forks. Once the filling is ready, gather some friends—shaping takes time.

5 Flour your countertop liberally. Split the dough in half. Keep one half covered, but place the other half on the floured surface. Use a rolling pin to flatten the dough about ⅛-inch thick. Punch out as many 3-inch dough circles as possible, using a round cookie cutter or a small glass. Squish the scraps into the remaining covered half of the dough.

6 Place about a tablespoon of filling in the center of one circle of dough. Fold the dough over the filling and press the edges to create a dumpling. The stickiness should ensure a tight seal. Lay the pierogi on a floured surface and use a fork to squish the edges together. Keep going until you run out of circles, then repeat with the remaining dough and filling.

7 Once you've formed all your pierogi, bring a pot of water to a boil over high heat. Add 12 pierogi to the water and let them cook until they rise to the surface, about 1 minute. Pull out the boiled pierogi with a spoon, bring the water back to a boil, and repeat with batches of the remaining pierogi.

8 If you're planning to freeze some of the pierogi, let them cool down and then put them in freezer bags with the air squeezed out. I usually do 12 to a bag, but you can portion them out in whatever way suits you. They will keep for at least 6 months.

9 You can eat the pierogi just boiled, but I prefer them fried afterward. Melt the butter in a pan over medium heat, then fry up as many pierogi as you want. (Six per person is plenty.) Flip them every few minutes until they're browned on all sides. Serve with scallions and a dollop of sour cream.

Dumplings

My friend Raffaella comes from a huge family and fondly recalls making dumplings with her sisters growing up. (Her brothers only helped eat them.) Dumplings are a great way to use up veggies that aren't fresh anymore. Minced and stuffed inside a dumpling, they come back to life! MAKES 60 DUMPLINGS

DOUGH

4 cups all-purpose flour, plus more for shaping the dough

1 teaspoon salt

2 eggs

VEGGIE FILLING

3 cups finely chopped broccoli

2 cups grated carrot

8 ounces firm tofu, crumbled

2 tablespoons soy sauce

1 teaspoon toasted sesame oil

2 scallions, chopped

2 eggs

PORK FILLING

1 pound ground pork or sausage, cooked or raw

3 cups finely chopped collards, chard, spinach, or scallions

2 tablespoons soy sauce

1 teaspoon toasted sesame oil

2 scallions, chopped

2 eggs

1 Mix the flour and salt in a large bowl. Make a crater in the middle, crack in the eggs, and add 1 cup of water. Use one hand like a shovel to mix the dough into a shaggy mass. If it seems too dry, add a few drops of water. Knead the dough for a minute, then cover it with plastic wrap or a damp towel and let it rest for 30 minutes to 2 hours.

2 In a large bowl, mix your desired filling ingredients.

3 Once the dough has rested, split it into 4 chunks. Dust your countertop with flour, then roll the first piece of dough into a log. Cover the other pieces so they don't dry out.

4 Cut the log into 15 equal slices, then form one of the slices into a flat disk with your hands. With a rolling pin, flatten the disk into an almost paper-thin circle about the size of a drink coaster.

5 Place a heaping tablespoon of filling in the center of the dough. Lift all the edges to meet in the middle, then pinch it closed like a little parcel. If the dough won't stick to itself, wet your fingertips and dab the edges.

6 Repeat until you run out of either filling or dough. Ask for help from family or friends—one person can roll while the others fill and cook.

7 Now, a tough decision: Steam, fry, or boil?

To steam them, spread a small amount of oil in a large pan. Fill the pan with dumplings—as many as you can fit without them sticking to each other. Turn the heat to medium and let them sizzle for a minute. Once the dough has absorbed most of the oil, add about ½ cup of water, then quickly cover with a lid. The water will splatter and sizzle. Leave the lid on for about a minute to steam the dumplings, then turn the heat to low and remove the lid. Cook until the water evaporates, then turn off the heat. Your dumplings should be steamed on top with crispy, brown bottoms.

To pan-fry them, follow the technique above, but use more oil. Skip the water and the lid entirely. Just keep frying! Once the dumplings are golden on one side, flip them to fry on the other side. This method is awkward with parcel-style dumplings but works well for other shapes (such as a pierogi shape, page 138), so plan accordingly.

To boil them, drop the dumplings into a pot of boiling water. When they rise to the top, they're ready to eat, usually in 1 or 2 minutes.

PANTRY

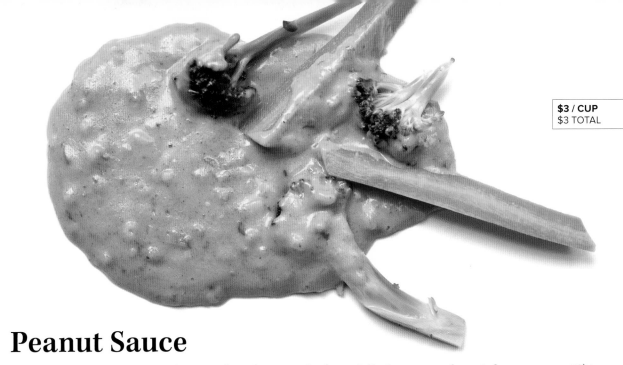

Peanut Sauce

This is my go-to dipping sauce for everything from veggies (especially the cornmeal crusted ones on page 72) to flatbread, to shrimp. But it's versatile enough to make a great marinade or coating for chicken or fish. My fridge is rarely without it. Try it, you'll see. **MAKES 1 CUP**

1 jalapeño pepper or other chile (remove seeds for less heat), or 2 tablespoons chile paste

3 cloves garlic

1 shallot or small onion

1 teaspoon vegetable oil

½ to 1 cup coconut milk

½ cup sugar-free peanut butter

1 tablespoon soy sauce

ADDITIONS

1 teaspoon ground turmeric

1 tablespoon brown sugar

½ teaspoon sesame oil

1 Finely chop the jalapeño, garlic, and shallot, or use a food processor to make them into a paste. (If you're using chile paste instead of a fresh pepper, add it in Step 2.)

2 Add the oil to a saucepan over medium heat. Once it's warm, sauté the pepper and garlic until fragrant, about 2 to 3 minutes. Add the ½ cup of coconut milk, turmeric, and chile paste, if using.

3 Let everything come to a boil, then turn the heat down to low. Stir in the peanut butter, soy sauce, and brown sugar and sesame oil, if using. If the sauce is too thick, add more coconut milk to thin it out. Once the mixture is well combined, taste it and add whatever you think it needs, concentrating on the salt and spices in particular.

$0.75 / CUP
$2.25 TOTAL

Salsa

Summertime salsas combine a load of fresh tomatoes with smaller amounts of choice vegetables and fruit. Apart from its usual use on tortilla chips and tacos, this salsa is a wonderful topping for fish or chicken, as a sauce for cold noodles, or as a finishing touch on a savory breakfast. If you aren't a fan of cilantro, substitute another herb; mint, savory, or lemon balm work well. MAKES 3 CUPS

½ medium onion, finely chopped

2 cups chopped tomatoes

1 jalapeño pepper, finely chopped (remove seeds for less heat)

juice of 1 lime

¼ cup finely chopped fresh cilantro

salt and pepper, to taste

ADDITIONS

chopped mango, peach, plum, or pineapple

beans

corn

finely chopped garlic

chipotle chiles in adobo instead of the jalapeño

1 If you like raw onion, skip ahead to Step 2. Otherwise, take the edge off by sautéing the onion with a bit of water in a pan over medium heat. The onion is ready once the water has boiled off.

2 Mix the onion, tomato, pepper, lime juice, cilantro, salt, and pepper in a bowl. Be sure to add enough salt and pepper!

3 Taste the salsa. You're looking for a balance of spicy from the jalapeño pepper, sweet from the tomatoes, and bright and fresh from the herbs and lime juice. If something's out of balance, add more of the appropriate ingredient to bring it back into balance.

4 Store in an airtight container in the fridge. Fresh salsa won't last as long as store-bought salsa because it doesn't have any preservatives, but it's so tasty that I'm sure you'll finish it fast!

FOR A WINTER VERSION, use canned tomatoes and heat everything but the lime juice on the stovetop for 5 minutes to marry the flavors. Finish with the lime juice and store.

Tzatziki

This classic yogurt sauce uses cucumbers in a way you might not have thought of before. Straining the yogurt and cucumber intensifies the flavor but, if you're in a hurry, skip the straining steps and just mix the ingredients together. MAKES 2 CUPS

1 large cucumber

1 teaspoon salt

2 cups yogurt

2 tablespoons chopped fresh dill

2 scallions, finely chopped

1 clove garlic, finely chopped (optional)

salt and pepper

1 Grate the cucumber and place it in a sieve over a large bowl. Add the salt and mix it around. Leave it for 30 minutes to 2 hours, occasionally pressing the cucumber gently into the sieve to get the liquid out. The salt will help leach the water out of the cucumber.

2 Line another sieve (or the same one, cleaned) with a paper towel or cheesecloth. Place it over a large bowl and pour the yogurt into it. You can leave it for as little as 1 hour on the counter or overnight in the fridge. The longer you leave it, the thicker it will get. This is how Greek yogurt is made!

3 Mix the yogurt with the strained cucumber, dill, scallions, and garlic, if using, and taste. Season with salt and pepper and add more dill or scallions to taste.

4 Enjoy on sandwiches, as a dip, with pita or chips, or over meatballs, kebabs, or anything spicy.

Raita

This traditional Indian yogurt sauce is simple and surprisingly tasty. Spoon it onto Chana Masala (page 109), Potato and Kale Rolls (page 116), or anything spicy to cool things down. This recipe is extremely loose—just stir some of your favorite chopped vegetables into yogurt and add salt and pepper. Use this as a stepping-stone to develop your signature raita. **MAKES 2 CUPS**

$1.25 / CUP
$2.50 TOTAL

1 cup yogurt
1 cup chopped cucumber
½ cup chopped tomato
¼ cup chopped red onion
1 teaspoon ground cumin
½ teaspoon cayenne pepper
2 tablespoons chopped fresh cilantro
salt and pepper

ADDITIONS
1 tablespoon grated ginger
2 tablespoons mint
¼ cup chickpeas
cooked spinach

1 Stir all the ingredients together in a medium-size bowl. Add salt and pepper to taste.

2 Store the raita in a covered container in the fridge until you're ready to use it. It will keep for up to 3 days.

ideas
FLAVOR

Many of the recipes in this collection can be easily modified to your taste. Learning to cook with different spices, herbs, and aromatics will instantly elevate your cooking and open up new and interesting possibilities. Although spices last a reasonably long time, they do grow stale and lose their intensity after a couple of months. When you experiment, buy small amounts of new spices in the bulk aisle and go for larger quantities of the spices you use most often.

Try the flavor combinations below on bland basics like rice, roasted chicken, vegetables, and potatoes. Starchy potatoes are almost the perfect flavor sponge.

Mix spices into butter, add them to popcorn, or sprinkle them on toast. In short, experiment!

GARLIC

Garlic! You should always have this around. Cheap and flavorful, it goes well with almost everything. Try sautéing vegetables, especially bitter green ones like broccoli and Brussels sprouts, with the following flavors, or pack the flavors into a creamy dressing over arugula or mustard greens. Any would make a great base for a pasta sauce, or bring a spark to plain rice or barley. Oh, and shellfish—did I mention shellfish?

- garlic and lemon zest

- garlic and fresh basil, fresh parsley, or rosemary

- garlic, onion, and ginger (heat with olive oil as the base for a stir-fry)

- garlic, anchovy, and chile flakes

CITRUS

The strongest lemon flavor comes not from the juice, but from the essential oils trapped in the bright, top layer of skin. Ditto for limes and oranges. If you want something to really taste like citrus, try adding just a touch of finely grated zest. It's very strong, though, so be careful with it. I add lemon zest to my tomato sauce, lime zest to pork tacos, and orange zest to dressing. Citrus brings out other flavors almost as well as salt.

- orange, lemon, and lime zests

- lime zest, coconut, and chile flakes

- orange zest, scallions, and fresh cilantro

- lime zest and chipotle powder

- lemon zest and fresh mint (amazing with cucumbers or watermelon)

HERBAL

Try sprinkling these classic combinations on roasted root vegetables or rub them all over a chicken before you roast it.

- sage, rosemary, and thyme

- sage and garlic (incredible with winter squash)

- paprika and fresh dill

- fennel seeds and fresh parsley

Fennel seeds—sweet and a little licorice-y—will be a familiar flavor to Italian sausage lovers, but it's not especially common in North America. Try them in a salad or in a blend with other spices. They bring out the flavors around them.

EARTHY

You want to get serious about spices? Try these South Asian combinations and don't be shy with them!

- ginger, cinnamon, and black pepper

Except for the pepper, the flavors above might seem like sweet spices, but they are wonderful in rice pilaf and with winter root vegetables. Add these to tea along with some cardamom for a traditional masala chai.

- cardamom, coriander, and bay leaf

- cumin seeds, coriander seeds, and mustard seeds

For one of the best stir-fries you'll ever have, heat a teaspoon each of the above in a dry skillet until you smell them, then add vegetables.

SWEET

If you're a baker, get yourself some of these lovely sweet spices to enliven all your standard favorite breads, cakes, and cookies. You can even add them to tea if you get adventurous. Try to get whole nutmeg rather than pre-ground. You'll be amazed at the difference that just a tiny grating of the fresh stuff will add to your food.

- cinnamon, ginger powder, nutmeg, and clove

- lemon zest and thyme (savory flavors that are incredible in a simple shortbread cookie)

- orange zest and cocoa powder

- lime and coconut

- green cardamom and vanilla

Try to get whole cardamom pods, smash the green pods and remove the black seeds in the center. Their aroma is much stronger when fresh rather than pre-ground. However, pre-ground cardamom is still fine in baked goods—you

may just need to use a little more of it to get the full flavor. The whole pods are lovely in rice and tea as well, so track some down if you're a cardamom fan.

MAKE YOUR OWN SPICE BLENDS

Some common spice blends can be made easily at home. For instance, instead of buying pre-made chili powder, make your own blend of cumin, cayenne pepper, garlic powder, oregano, and paprika. The spices included in the ingredients for Dark and Spicy Chili (with the exception of cocoa powder) make a chili powder that can be substituted for the pre-made stuff.

Curry powder is a bunch of South Asian spices blended together, and there are many, many varieties of curry blends—usually, some combination of turmeric, coriander, cumin, and chile powder.

Garam masala, another spice blend that is essential to Indian cooking, is most often made with similar spices, but rarely includes chile powder. Try pre-made curry and garam masala blends to start, and work your way up to making your own.

Don't buy pumpkin pie spice. It's usually stale and bland. Just hit your pumpkin pie or cookies with a mix of cinnamon, nutmeg, ground ginger, and a little clove.

AVOID SOME DRIED HERBS

Dried oregano, dried thyme, and dried rosemary add a lot of flavor to chili, soups, and roasted vegetables. However, don't bother with dried basil, dried cilantro, dried dill, and definitely not dried mint, unless you particularly like them and can't afford to get them fresh. They lose almost all their magic when dried.

SALT

Salt is essential to bringing out the natural flavor in any food and should be used alongside any other flavors you choose. If something doesn't taste quite right, the answer most of the time is to add a bit more salt. Granted, those with health conditions where sodium levels can cause harm should watch their intake! If you can't use much salt in your diet, try replacing it with spice, a squeeze of citrus juice, or a sprinkling of citrus zest.

IT'S EASY TO MAKE a basic salad dressing, so you should never have to buy it pre-made. Simply follow the instructions for the basic vinaigrette on page 44, and add any of the flavor combinations suggested here to experiment. The ones under citrus are the best place to start.

Spice Oil

Use this spice oil on salads, in cold noodle dishes, or on roasted or sautéed vegetables. You can get all of the spices at most Asian grocery stores. MAKES 1 CUP

1 clove garlic

1 cup olive or vegetable oil

2 tablespoons chile flakes or chopped dried red chiles

1 teaspoon Sichuan or regular peppercorns

1 star anise

½ teaspoon cumin seeds

¼ teaspoon salt

1 Use the side of a knife to crush the garlic clove, and peel it when it cracks open.

2 Place the crushed garlic in a small pot and add the olive oil, chile flakes, peppercorns, star anise, cumin seeds, and salt. Warm the mixture over low heat, until it starts to bubble gently and you can hear a bit of a sizzle, about 10 minutes. Turn off the heat. You don't want it to be so hot that the spices start to cook or fry.

3 Put the covered pot in the fridge for 4 to 8 hours.

4 Taste the oil. If it isn't strongly spicy, let it infuse for a few more hours. Once it's ready, strain the oil through a sieve to remove the spices. Store in a jar in the fridge for up to a week.

IF YOU DON'T HAVE A SIEVE, place a lid over the pot and carefully pour the oil out sideways to strain it. Allow a small opening between the lid and the pot so the oil can escape while the spices are left behind.

Roti

These flatbreads are a staple in many parts of India. They're quick to make and very tasty when fresh. Enjoy them with a curried filling, dip them into soups or stews, or wrap them around eggs at breakfast. **MAKES 16 ROTI**

2 cups whole-wheat flour (see box)
1 teaspoon salt
1 cup water
vegetable oil, for coating your hands

1 Mix the flour, salt, and water in a small bowl using one clean hand. It should form a fairly moist dough. Knead until smooth—anywhere from 2 to 5 minutes—and form into a ball. Cover with a damp towel or paper towel and set aside for 10 minutes to an hour.

2 Rub a small amount of oil onto your hands to make it easier to handle the dough. Divide the dough into 16 small balls.

3 Sprinkle a countertop with flour and place one piece of dough in the middle. Cover the ball with flour so it doesn't stick to the surface, then gently roll it out with a rolling pin (or a bottle if you're in a pinch) until it's thin and flat, about ⅛ inch thick. As you roll the dough, unstick it from your counter and flip it over. To make it round, roll straight in front of you, then turn the dough 90 degrees and roll out again.

4 Place a nonstick skillet over medium heat (cast-iron is best). Once the pan is hot, add the roti and cook until the dough lifts away from the pan around the edges and small bubbles form, 1 to 2 minutes. Flip the bread over and cook the other side. You want to see light brown bubbles all over the dough. Don't let it get too dark, though, as this will make the roti too crunchy to use for rolls. Repeat until you run out of dough.

5 Keep the roti under a towel on the counter or in a warm oven until ready to serve.

WHOLE-WHEAT DURUM FLOUR, sometimes called *roti* or *chapati* flour, can be found in Indian grocery stores and is the best flour to use for this recipe. You can use regular whole-wheat flour as well, but if you want to make this recipe often, consider a special trip to get roti flour!

$0.03 / ROTI
$0.50 TOTAL

Flour Tortillas

Homemade tortillas are a bit of work, but they're totally worth it. With practice, you'll get quicker and enjoy the process as much as the results. **MAKES 24 SMALL TORTILLAS**

1¼ cups all-purpose flour, plus more
    for shaping the dough

1¼ cups whole-wheat flour

2½ teaspoons baking powder

1 teaspoon salt

⅓ cup clarified butter or lard,
    at room temperature (see box)

1 cup hot water

LARD is more traditional, but I prefer clarified butter (which is just butter with the milk solids removed). Even regular butter will work. You can also buy ghee from an Indian grocer and use that.

---

1 Whisk together the flours, baking powder, and salt in a large bowl. Add the clarified butter. Using your fingers, work the butter into the flour until the mixture looks like moist crumbs. Add the hot water—not boiling, just hot—and form the dough with your hands. Leave it in the bowl for an hour, covered by plastic wrap or a moist towel.

2 Roll the dough into 24 small balls, then cover them again.

3 Lightly flour your countertop. Gently flatten one dough ball with your palm, then roll it out with a rolling pin. Flip it over to make sure it doesn't stick to the counter; add more flour if it does stick. Once the dough is a nice, thin, 5- to 6-inch circle, set it aside under a moist towel.

4 Once you've rolled out one or two tortillas, put a nonstick or cast-iron pan over medium-high heat. Let it get nice and hot. Place a tortilla in the pan. Once it starts to dry up around the edges, flip it over with a spatula, then gently press it down to give it some color underneath.

5 Once the tortilla has brown spots on both sides, remove it from the pan and continue with the next. Work quickly! As you wait for each tortilla to cook, roll out more. You'll get better at this part with practice.

6 If you're serving the tortillas soon, place them in a warm oven to keep them pliable. If they're for later in the day, pile them under a cloth while you finish making them. Once you're done, wrap them in aluminum foil and put them in the fridge. Heat them in the oven before serving.

Pizza Dough

There are two ways to make pizza dough: the fast way and the slow way. They're the same amount of work, just with different wait times. The slow method is convenient for a weekday with a little preparation—make it the night before you plan to make pizza, pop it in the fridge, and then pull it out to rise a few hours before dinner. If you're organized enough to make the slow dough, I recommend taking the extra time: It tastes best, and is much softer and easier to stretch. **MAKES 4 INDIVIDUAL PIZZAS**

3 cups all-purpose flour or bread
    flour, plus more for shaping
    the dough

1½ teaspoons salt

½ to 1 teaspoon instant yeast

1 tablespoon olive oil, plus more for
    coating the bowl

1¼ cups water, at room temperature

Fast Method

1 Measure out the flour, salt, and 1 teaspoon of yeast into a big bowl. Mix in the oil with your hands, crumbling until the texture is a bit sandy, then add the water. Keep mixing until the dough comes together.

2 Lightly flour your countertop. Gently stretch and fold the dough to knead it, pushing against the countertop over and over. Massage the dough until it becomes smooth and elastic, about 5 to 7 minutes. The dough will be smooth but quite wet.

3 Add a small amount of oil to a bowl. Place your dough ball in the bowl and cover with plastic wrap. Let it rise for 1½ to 3 hours, depending on the warmth of your kitchen. It's done rising when it has doubled in size. Now you're ready to make pizza! For rolling instructions, see page 152.

Slow Method

1 Follow Steps 1 and 2 of the fast method, but add only ½ teaspoon of yeast to the flour mixture. Use very cold water instead of room temperature.

2 Add a small amount of oil to a bowl. Place your dough ball in the bowl and cover with plastic wrap. Put it into the fridge overnight. Letting the yeast work overnight creates a better flavor; it also makes the dough more elastic and easy to work with.

3 The next day, 2 to 3 hours before you want to bake your pizzas, remove the dough from the fridge to return to room temperature. Now you're ready to make pizza! See page 120 for how to roll it out.

$0.20 / CRUST
$0.80 TOTAL

method
CROUTONS OR BREADCRUMBS

I am constantly haunted by crusts of hard, several-days-old bread that I have neglected. Luckily, there are plenty of delicious solutions that help those crusts avoid the trash can. Croutons and breadcrumbs will keep for ages in a sealed container on the counter, and when you have them around, you'll find yourself using them everywhere—and perhaps even finding excuses to make a salad. You can make this with any amount of bread.

bread

butter or vegetable oil, as needed

salt and pepper, to taste

1 Prepare the bread. For croutons, cut the bread into cubes. For breadcrumbs, mince the loaf with a knife, tear it apart, or throw small chunks of bread into a food processor. If the bread is too hard to cut, wrap it in a kitchen towel, sprinkle some water on the towel, and microwave for 20 to 30 seconds. This will restore just enough moisture to let you cut the bread easily.

2 Place a large pan on the stove over medium heat. Add enough butter—usually at least a tablespoon—to coat the bottom of the pan. **Melt the butter.**

3 Working in batches, add the bread and toss it gently until it's coated in butter. Let the bread sit for 2 minutes, then flip the pieces over. Keep tossing and turning, leaving it for a minute or so at a time, until the bread is brown all over. Add more butter as needed. The bread cubes may get kind of dry, and a little more fat will help them brown more evenly. Sprinkle with salt and pepper. It is basically impossible, unless you are very patient (which I am not), to get every side of the cubes browned, so just get them generally looking good and toasty and then take them off the heat. Taste one and add more salt and pepper, if you need to.

4 Use the breadcrumbs or croutons immediately, or store them in a sealed container after letting them cool off.

> **FOR BREADCRUMBS,** if you like, you can go oil free: just toast whole slices of bread and then crush or process them into small pieces.

Fresh Pasta

When a reader, Jeanne, asked for a good pasta dish, I decided to show her how to create it from scratch. Sure, making pasta by hand requires elbow grease and a good rolling pin, but you'll be surprised at how simple, cheap, and tasty it is. If an Italian grandmother can do it, so can you! Because fresh pasta is so wonderful, the sauce you pair it with doesn't need to be complicated. Try it with Best Tomato Sauce (page 127) or Chorizo and White Bean Ragù (page 128) and a little cheese. SERVES 1 VERY HUNGRY PERSON

MULTIPLY THIS RECIPE by the number of people you are serving. The stated quantities are a useful ratio, but they produce big portions.

¾ cup all-purpose or bread flour, plus more for shaping the dough

1 egg

olive or vegetable oil

salt

1 Put the flour in a bowl. Make a crater in the center of the flour and crack the egg into it. Mix with your hands. The egg takes a while to release all its moisture, so don't panic if things are dry at first. If, after mixing for about a minute, the dough still seems excessively dry, add a teaspoon of water. Keep mixing until you develop a stiff dough that is quite dry. The dryness makes it easier to roll out and keeps the noodles from sticking together when you cook them.

2 Add a small amount of oil to a bowl. Place the dough in the bowl, cover with a moist towel or plastic wrap, and let rest for 1 to 2 hours.

3 Once an hour (or more) has passed, you should notice a marked change in the dough. The egg will have released its moisture to form a pale yellow, smooth, pliable dough. Knead it again to create a smooth ball.

4 Tear or slice the dough into manageable pieces—usually as many as the number of people you're feeding. Dust your countertop heavily with flour, then use a rolling pin to make the dough as thin as you can. Rolling it out will take a while because it's tough and stretchy. Try to get it thin enough to see light through it. The thinner the dough, the quicker it will cook, but don't make the dough so thin that it tears.

5 By the time the pasta is rolled out, it should be dry enough to avoid sticking to itself. If it's still moist, let it sit for a few minutes.

6 Boil a pot of heavily salted water.

7 Slice the dough into whatever size noodles you like. If you fold the dough over itself a few times, it's easy to make the noodles a consistent size. Shake the cut noodles on a tray with a bit of flour to keep them from sticking.

8 When the pot of water has come to a boil, add the pasta. Fresh pasta takes as little as 30 seconds to cook, if the noodles are thin. It's ready when it changes color and starts to float. Taste a noodle after they start to float to see if it's cooked. If not, let it cook a little longer.

9 Drain and serve immediately. Uncooked pasta will keep, wrapped in plastic or spread out on a covered baking sheet, for up to 2 days in the fridge. Dust it with enough flour to keep it from sticking to itself.

$0.35 / SERVING
$0.35 TOTAL

Ricotta

To transform regular milk into something truly special, make your own ricotta. It's a neat recipe to do with kids because it's simple, yet the transformation of the milk is dramatic. Try this in lasagna or anywhere else you would usually use ricotta, but be sure to enjoy a little of it on its own to appreciate its full deliciousness. I love it best on toast (shocking!) with a sprinkling of pesto or chopped herbs on top to cut the richness of the cheese. Save the whey to use in soups instead of broth. **MAKES 1½ CUPS**

½ gallon whole milk
1 cup heavy cream
1 teaspoon salt
3 tablespoons distilled white vinegar
   or lemon juice

ADDITIONS
fresh herbs
dried herbs
any spice combination (page 149)

1 Place the milk, cream, and salt in a large, heavy-bottomed pot and bring just to a boil. When just one bubble comes up to the top, add the vinegar, give it a stir, and turn off the heat. The vinegar will create a disturbance and the whey and cream will begin to separate.

2 Meanwhile, line a sieve with cheesecloth or two layers of paper towels and place over a large bowl.

3 Leave the mixture in the pot for 5 minutes, then stir to separate the cheese and the whey completely. They should be two distinct parts of the mixture. If some of it is still milky, add another tablespoon of vinegar, stir, and let it sit for a few more minutes.

4 Pour your ricotta mixture into the cheesecloth-lined sieve with the bowl underneath to catch the whey. Leave for 30 minutes to drain.

5 The cheesecloth will be full of a crumbly white cheese. That's your ricotta! Taste it and add more salt if it needs it, or add herbs or spices.

6 Eat immediately, or pack into an airtight container and store in the fridge. The ricotta will keep for about 3 days.

$0.20 / SERVING
$0.40 TOTAL

ideas
RAINBOW RICE

Here are three quick ways to make plain rice a little more exciting. An early reader, Charles, said he loves rice with vegetables, but these treatments work for grains other than rice as well—everything from quinoa to barley to farro. Vegetables are a great way to liven up the usual rice and beans.

Plain Rice

SERVES 2

2 cups water
1 cup rice
2 pinches of salt

To make plain rice, pour the water into a pot and add the uncooked rice and salt. That'll be enough for two generous portions, or three or four smaller servings. With the lid off, bring to a low boil over medium heat. Turn down the heat to low and put the lid on slightly askew, so that the steam can escape. Cook for about 20 minutes, until the water is all gone and the rice is fluffy.

❶ Green Rice

$1 SERVING / $2 TOTAL

1 cup frozen spinach, beet greens, chard, or fresh parsley

Chop the spinach as much as you like. The more finely chopped, the more it will disperse into the rice. Cook as directed for plain rice, but after cooking for 15 minutes, mix the spinach into the rice. Cook with the lid off for the last 5 minutes. Adding the spinach at the end keeps it lush and bright, rather than sad and overcooked.

❷ Orange Rice

$1 SERVING / $2 TOTAL

1 cup canned winter squash, pumpkin, or sweet potato puree

Stir the squash with 1½ cups of water in a bowl, then pour it into a pot with the rice and salt. (You can also use frozen, boiled, or sautéed squash.) Cook as directed for plain rice.

❸ Red Rice

$1 SERVING / $2 TOTAL

1 cup canned tomatoes, pureed

Stir the tomatoes with 1½ cups of water, then pour into a pot with the rice and salt. Cook as directed for plain rice.

method
HOW TO COOK DRIED BEANS

This method works for cooking any kind of beans in any amount. Make a large batch on a Sunday and use them in meals throughout the week. The only thing to keep in mind is that the older and bigger they are, the longer they take to cook. Some may take as long as 4 hours. If you eat a lot of beans, consider investing in a pressure cooker, which will cut down on the boiling time.

ADDITIONS

bay leaf

bouquet garni of favorite tough
  herbs

dried herbs and spices

onion

garlic

chiles

ginger, sliced

1 The best way to prepare dried beans is to **soak them in water overnight**. The next day, drain and rinse the beans thoroughly before cooking them in fresh water. If you don't have the opportunity to soak the beans ahead of time, you can make up for it: Cover the beans with water, then bring them to a boil in a large pot. After 10 minutes, take them off the heat and drain them.

2 Place the drained beans in a large pot and cover with fresh water. Include any additions you desire.

3 Bring to a boil over medium heat, then turn down the heat so that the beans simmer gently. Put a lid on the pot, but leave it askew so the water doesn't boil over.

4 Check on the beans every half hour or so, being sure to keep them covered with water if it boils away.

5 Beans take vastly different lengths of time to become tender. The older and bigger they are, the longer they take to cook. Very old, very large beans can take as long as 4 hours. If you are making refried beans or beans for a soup or stew, don't worry about overcooking them—it's fine if they're mushy. If you want to maintain their shape and integrity, however, monitor them closely once they're nearly done, after a couple of hours.

6 Once the beans are tender, you can drain them or leave them in their cooking water, depending on what you're using them for. Remove and discard the additions, if necessary, and add salt to taste— they will need a fair bit!

method
PICKLE PRIMER

Pickles made from cucumbers are undeniably America's favorite kind of pickle. But pickled carrots, beets, asparagus, onions, and cauliflower are delicious as well. Pickled vegetables are not only incredibly delicious—they are also a great way to preserve vegetables when you have an unexpected bounty that you don't want to go to waste. A friend left five pounds of zucchini on your doorstep? Pickle it! You might also want to consider pickles for holiday gifts. I get requests for them every year!

The form of pickling I'm describing isn't proper, long-term preserving or canning. That process is worth learning, but it requires specialized equipment. Here we're learning the quick method to create tangy, flavorful, quick pickles that blow any store-bought pickles away.

ESSENTIALS

vegetables (cucumbers, zucchini, cauliflower, carrots, beets, asparagus, onions, peppers, or string beans)

1-quart mason jars (see box)

ADDITIONS TO THE JAR

sprigs of dill

garlic cloves, quartered

BRINE

1 cup distilled white vinegar

1 cup water

1 tablespoon salt

1 teaspoon mustard seeds

1 teaspoon dill seeds

1 bay leaf

ADDITIONS TO THE BRINE

1 or 2 dried chiles, crushed

cinnamon stick

2 whole cloves

½ teaspoon coriander seeds

½ teaspoon allspice berries

½ teaspoon fennel seeds

½ teaspoon celery seeds

1 tablespoon sugar

MULTIPLY THIS RECIPE by the number of quarts of brine you want to end up with. The quantities below are a ratio—they will make roughly enough brine to fill a 1 quart mason jar (depending on how tightly packed it is with vegetables). You can adjust the ratio according to how many vegetables you have and how many jars you want to fill. I suggest making at least 6 quarts at once if you have the space in the fridge. It's more efficient to make a large batch and, trust me, they will be popular.

---

1 Cut up the vegetables however you like. Smaller pieces will pickle faster because the brine takes less time to penetrate them. I generally go with bite-size pieces, or long strips if making cucumber pickles. You can also add any other vegetables or herbs for flavor.

2 Fill the jars with the vegetables.

3 Make the brine: Pour the vinegar, water, and salt into a pot. Put in any other additions. If you don't maintain a spice collection, you can buy pickling mix in the spice aisle of most grocery stores. Instead of the seeds and bay leaf, add 1 tablespoon of pickling mix to the water, vinegar, and salt. And for sweet pickles, add about 1 tablespoon of sugar.

4 Bring the brine to a boil and turn the heat down to low. **Simmer for 10 minutes.**

5 Pour the hot liquid over the vegetables in the jars. If you don't have enough, don't panic. Simply make more using the ratio in the brine ingredients list. If you've run out of spices, just skip them.

6 Place the lids over the jars. Don't screw them on tightly until the jars have come to room temperature. Once the jars have cooled completely, screw on the lids and put the jars in the fridge.

7 Leave the pickles for 2 weeks to let the brine do its work. After 2 weeks, eat them!

IDEALLY, you'll have glass jars with tight-fitting screw-top lids. You can usually find jars for canning at hardware stores or many grocery stores, but another kind of glass jar or an old pickle jar will do in a pinch. Mason jars can be used over and over and I use them to house things like dried beans and grains, so they are very useful and inexpensive storage.

DRINKS
AND
DESSERTS

method
AGUA FRESCA

Refreshing, hydrating, and beautiful, these drinks are great at a party, and they can help you use up fruit before it goes bad. Use this as a starting point for developing your own favorite.

2 cups chopped fruit

4 cups water

ADDITIONS

1 teaspoon vanilla extract

squeeze of citrus juice

sugar

mint leaves

leaves of other herbs

VARIATIONS

blueberry and lemon

cucumber and lemon

mango and lime

melon

orange

papaya and pineapple

peach and vanilla

strawberry and mint

1 For a very lightly flavored agua fresca, just mix the fruit and water together. Done! Obviously, if you want more fruit flavor, then use less water; for a more subtle flavor, use more water.

2 Serve over ice. Try some of the variations I've suggested or whatever fruits you like! If you store this in the fridge, it'll keep for about 3 days or up to a week, depending on the fruit.

I USUALLY RUN MY AGUA FRESCA THROUGH THE BLENDER. If you want the drink to be clear, strain the pulpy leftovers of the fruit after blending. If you're using blueberries or oranges or other fruit with a skin, you'll almost certainly want to strain it. For some fruits, you can also choose to leave the pulp: in the case of melons, the pulp purees so smoothly that you barely notice it.

ideas
SMOOTHIES

I have four types of smoothies here, but, of course, once you get the hang of it, there are many more flavor combinations to be made. Frozen fruit is perfect for smoothies. Or, use overripe fruit that you wouldn't eat otherwise. Add a teaspoon of vanilla extract to any of these and they will seem incredibly professional. The frozen melon drinks, in particular, are a refreshing slushy-like treat on a hot summer day. Two—watermelon and honeydew—are pictured at right. (The mango lassi is not pictured.) **SERVES 2**

❶ Drinkable Yogurt

$0.50 SERVING / $1 TOTAL

½ cup yogurt, not Greek
½ cup fruit juice

If you like the grocery store's yogurt drinks, try making these at home for less! You don't even need to blend them—just add the yogurt and juice to a jar, then shake.

❷ Berry Smoothie

$1 SERVING / $2 TOTAL

½ cup yogurt, not Greek
1 cup frozen berries
milk or juice to thin as
    needed
1 teaspoon vanilla extract

Blend the yogurt, berries, a bit of milk, and vanilla until smooth, then adjust with more berries or milk to your taste.

❸ Melon Smoothie

$0.50 SERVING / $1 TOTAL

1 cup chopped frozen
    melon
½ cup water or juice
1 teaspoon vanilla extract

When you buy a melon, dice and freeze whatever you don't eat. Pull it out a cup at a time and blend it with a bit of water or juice and vanilla to thin it out. It's like a slushy, but better!

❹ Mango Lassi

$1 SERVING / $2 TOTAL

1 mango, peeled, pitted,
    and diced
1 cup yogurt, not Greek
milk to thin as needed

Blend the mango and yogurt together. If it's too thick to drink with a straw, add some milk to thin it out. A ripe and juicy mango combined with yogurt is often all you need. Be warned: If you make this for children, they will request it over and over.

Avocado Milkshake

John, the reader who introduced me to the silky magic of this milkshake, lives in California, where avocados are often less than a dollar. If you can find a similar deal, whip up a batch of these! **SERVES 2**

1 avocado, peeled and pitted

2 cups milk, coconut milk beverage, almond milk, or rice milk

1 teaspoon vanilla extract

1 tablespoon lime juice

pinch of salt

2 tablespoons sugar

Toss the avocado, milk, vanilla, lime juice, salt, and sugar into a blender and whiz them up! Let it go for a while so that the avocado breaks down and blends with the milk. Once the liquid is Kermit the Frog green, it's ready. Taste it and add more sugar or lime juice as needed.

> **IF YOUR AVOCADO ISN'T QUITE RIPE,** a bit more lime juice will bring out its flavor.

Fast Melon Sorbet

When you see lovely watermelons, honeydews, and cantaloupes on sale, buy them up. Eat half, then cube and freeze the other half. When you want a quick dessert or smoothie, pull out a bag of frozen melon and whip this up. **SERVES 4**

2 cups chopped frozen melon
½ cup plain yogurt
¼ cup sugar
1 teaspoon vanilla extract or lime juice (optional)

Add the melon, yogurt, sugar, and vanilla, if using, to a food processor or blender. Process or blend until just smooth. Don't blend too much, or the sorbet will become overly soft. Serve immediately or store in the freezer to enjoy later.

$0.60 / SERVING
$2.40 TOTAL

ideas
RICE PUDDING

Rice pudding is so simple to make—it's almost as easy as cooking plain rice. It's a wonderful make-ahead dessert if you have guests, and it can easily be dressed up with berries, nuts, or Caramelized Bananas (page 177). I've included a few variations, but please do experiment: Milk, rice, and sugar are a great canvas. Try switching out the sugar for honey, or stirring in a spoonful of cocoa powder, peanut butter, or coconut flakes. **SERVES 4**

Basic (Vanilla) Pudding

SERVES 4

½ cup long-grain rice
2 cups milk
½ cup sugar
⅛ teaspoon salt
2 teaspoons vanilla extract or ½ vanilla bean, seeds scraped

1 Place a pot over medium heat and add the rice, milk, sugar, and salt. Stir until the sugar is dissolved and then bring to a boil. Once the milk is just boiling, turn the heat down to low and simmer for 20 minutes. Place a lid slightly askew on the pot so the steam can escape.

2 Remove a grain of rice and taste it to see whether it's cooked. If it is soft and chewy all the way through, then it's done. If not, let it cook for a few more minutes. Once the rice is cooked, add the vanilla, and stir.

3 Remove the pudding from the heat and let it cool to room temperature. Let it chill in the fridge for 2 hours before serving. You can also eat it hot, but if you wait, the pudding will thicken in the fridge and have a more pleasing texture.

❶ Indian-Style
$0.65 SERVING / $2.60 TOTAL

½ cup basmati rice
2 cups milk
½ cup sugar
⅛ teaspoon salt
1 teaspoon cardamom
¼ cup chopped almonds or pistachios

Follow the instructions for vanilla rice pudding, but use basmati rice and add cardamom in place of the vanilla in Step 2. Top with chopped nuts.

❷ Pumpkin Pie
$0.60 SERVING / $2.40 TOTAL

½ cup long-grain rice
¾ cup canned or fresh pumpkin puree
2 cups milk
½ cup brown sugar
⅛ teaspoon salt
1 teaspoon ground cinnamon
½ teaspoon ground cloves
½ teaspoon ground ginger

Follow the instructions for vanilla rice pudding, but substitute brown sugar and add pumpkin, cinnamon, cloves, and ginger, and stir together before adding to the pot. Simmer for 25 minutes (instead of 20), stirring occasionally.

Coconut and Lime Brown Rice Pudding

Tangy, rich, creamy, and just a little chewy, this dessert may be a healthier alternative to the rice puddings on page 175, but it sure doesn't feel like a compromise. **SERVES 2**

½ cup short-grain brown rice

2 cups water

⅛ teaspoon salt

1 can (13.5 ounces) full-fat coconut milk

½ cup sugar

zest of 1 lime or orange

4 slices ginger, added with the coconut milk then removed before serving (optional)

1 Place a pot over medium heat. Add the rice, water, and salt. Bring to a boil, turn the heat down to low, and cook the rice for 35 minutes. Place a lid slightly askew on the pot so the steam can escape.

2 Dump the rice into a sieve to drain. It should be almost cooked, but not quite.

3 Add the coconut milk and sugar to the now-empty pot over medium heat. Stir and let cook until the sugar is dissolved.

4 Put the brown rice back in the pot and bring it to a boil over medium heat. Turn the heat down to low and simmer with the lid on for 15 more minutes. Test to make sure the rice is tender—if it's not, let it simmer for a few more minutes. Add the lime or orange zest and stir.

5 Remove the pudding from the heat and let it cool to room temperature. You can also eat it hot, but if you chill it for 2 hours before serving, it will thicken and have a more pleasing texture.

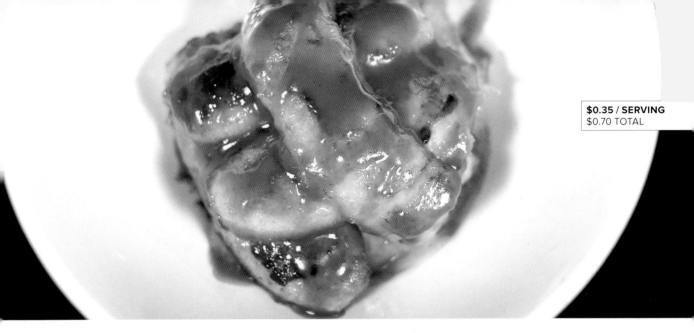

Caramelized Bananas

These bananas—cooked in just a bit of caramel—are crispy and gooey on the outside and almost like a soft pudding inside. Sweet, messy, and irresistible. SERVES 2

1 tablespoon butter

2 tablespoons brown sugar

2 bananas, peeled and split in half lengthwise

1 Melt the butter in a nonstick or cast-iron pan over medium-high heat. Add the sugar and let it melt into the butter for about 2 minutes. Stir once to create a smooth mixture.

2 Place the bananas flat-side down in the butter-sugar mixture, then cook until they become brown and sticky, about 2 minutes. Carefully flip them over and do the same on the other side.

3 Serve them as is or cut them into quarters. Drizzle any caramel left in the pan over the bananas. Serve with ice cream or on their own.

$0.25 / COOKIE
$10 TOTAL

Coconut Chocolate Cookies

This is a just-chewy-enough, just-crispy-enough, just-gooey-enough cookie that's perfect for a special treat.

MAKES APPROXIMATELY 40 COOKIES

⅔ cup shaved unsweetened coconut

1 cup (2 sticks) unsalted butter

2 cups all-purpose flour

1 teaspoon salt, plus extra for sprinkling

1 teaspoon baking soda

1½ cups firmly packed dark brown sugar

2 eggs

2 teaspoons vanilla extract

1½ cups chocolate chips

1 Preheat the oven to 350°F.

2 Spread the coconut in a thin, even layer on a baking sheet. Place it in the oven and bake until it's light brown, toasty, and aromatic, 5 to 8 minutes.

3 Melt the butter in a heavy-bottomed saucepan over low heat. Allow the melted butter to cool in the pan for a few minutes.

4 Stir together the flour, salt, and baking soda in a medium-size bowl.

5 Beat the brown sugar and melted butter together in a large bowl until smooth, about 2 minutes. Add the eggs and vanilla and beat until the mixture lightens in color, about 5 minutes. Add the flour mixture to the brown sugar mixture, a third at a time, until it forms a dark brown, homogeneous mass. Add the chocolate chips and toasted coconut and stir until just combined.

6 Place the dough in the fridge for 20 minutes. You can skip this step if you're in a hurry, but resting the dough in the fridge will help your cookies bake more evenly.

7 Lightly butter a baking sheet and scoop heaping tablespoons of dough onto it, leaving large spaces between each cookie so they have room to spread out. I usually do about 6 cookies per sheet. Just before putting the cookies into the oven, sprinkle them with salt.

8 Let the cookies bake until they're golden, 8 to 10 minutes. After you take them out of the oven, leave them on the baking sheet to set for 2 minutes, then move them to a wire rack to cool further. The cookies are very soft when they first come out of the oven, but they'll firm up quickly, so if you leave them on the sheet for 2 minutes, they'll transfer more easily. Don't stack the cookies until they're fully cooled.

9 Repeat Steps 7 and 8 until all the dough is used. Store the finished cookies in an airtight container for up to a week.

Peach Coffee Cake

Adapted from the apple cake often served during Rosh Hashanah, this coffee cake is simple and wonderful for dessert, with tea, or as a sweet breakfast. The juicy peaches add a ton of flavor. If you buy peaches in season, the cost can be quite reasonable. SERVES 12

1 cup (2 sticks) unsalted butter, at room temperature

6 peaches, pitted and cut into 8 slices each

juice of ½ lemon

1 teaspoon ground cinnamon

2 cups all-purpose flour

2 teaspoons baking powder

1⅓ cups plus 1 tablespoon firmly packed brown sugar

⅛ teaspoon salt

1 teaspoon vanilla extract

2 large eggs

> **THIS CAKE** is a great base for all kinds of fruit, from other stone fruit like plums, to apples, to berries. Anything but citrus or melons will work. Try frozen fruit if what you want is not in season.

1 Preheat the oven to 350°F.

2 Use the paper wrapping from the butter to lightly grease an 8- by 11-inch glass baking dish or 9-inch springform pan. Any shape will do as long as it is large enough. This cake doubles in size when it bakes.

3 Mix the peach slices, lemon juice, and cinnamon with your hands in a large bowl, making sure the peaches are well coated in cinnamon.

4 Stir together the flour and baking powder in a medium-size bowl, getting rid of any lumps.

5 Beat the butter, 1⅓ cups brown sugar, and salt in another large bowl, either with a wooden spoon or an electric mixer. Stop when the mixture is fluffy and has slightly lightened in color, about 5 minutes. Add the vanilla, then the eggs one at a time, fully mixing in the first before adding the second.

6 Add the flour mixture to the butter mixture, gently incorporating until it's smooth. (If you're using an electric mixer, switch to a wooden spoon.) The batter will be quite thick.

7 Spread half the batter over the bottom of the buttered pan. Evenly distribute 24 of the peach slices over the top. (There should be 48 in total.) Spread the other half of the batter over the peaches, then top with the rest of the peaches. Sprinkle with the remaining 1 tablespoon brown sugar and place the cake in the oven.

8 Bake until a knife inserted into the center comes out clean, about 1 hour.

$0.75 / SERVING
$9 TOTAL

CONVERSION TABLES

Please note that all conversions are approximate but close enough to be useful when converting from one system to another.

OVEN TEMPERATURES

Fahrenheit	Gas Mark	Celsius
250	½	120
275	1	140
300	2	150
325	3	160
350	4	180
375	5	190
400	6	200
425	7	220
450	8	230
475	9	240
500	10	260

NOTE: Reduce the temperature by 20°C (68°F) for fan-assisted ovens.

APPROXIMATE EQUIVALENTS

1 stick butter = 8 tbsp = 4 oz = ½ cup = 115 g

1 cup all-purpose presifted flour = 4.7 oz

1 cup granulated sugar = 8 oz = 220 g

1 cup firmly packed brown sugar = 6 oz = 220 g to 230 g

1 cup honey or syrup = 12 oz

1 cup grated cheese = 4 oz

1 cup dried beans = 6 oz

1 large egg = about 2 oz or about 3 tbsp

1 egg yolk = about 1 tbsp

1 egg white = about 2 tbsp

LIQUID CONVERSIONS

US	Imperial	Metric
2 tbsp	1 fl oz	30 ml
3 tbsp	1¼ fl oz	45 ml
¼ cup	2 fl oz	60 ml
⅔ cup	2½ fl oz	75 ml
⅓ cup + 1 tbsp	3 fl oz	90 ml
⅓ cup + 2 tbsp	3½ fl oz	100 ml
½ cup	4 fl oz	125 ml
⅔ cup	5 fl oz	150 ml
¾ cup	6 fl oz	175 ml
¾ cup + 2 tbsp	7 fl oz	200 ml
1 cup	8 fl oz	250 ml
1 cup + 2 tbsp	9 fl oz	275 ml
1¼ cups	10 fl oz	300 ml
1⅓ cups	11 fl oz	325 ml
1½ cups	12 fl oz	350 ml
1⅔ cups	13 fl oz	375 ml
1¾ cups	14 fl oz	400 ml
1¾ cups + 2 tbsp	15 fl oz	450 ml
2 cups (1 pint)	16 fl oz	500 ml
2½ cups	20 fl oz (1 pint)	600 ml
3¾ cups	1½ pints	900 ml
4 cups	1¾ pints	1 liter

WEIGHT CONVERSIONS

US/UK	Metric	US/UK	Metric
½ oz	15 g	7 oz	200 g
1 oz	30 g	8 oz	250 g
1½ oz	45 g	9 oz	275 g
2 oz	60 g	10 oz	300 g
2½ oz	75 g	11 oz	325 g
3 oz	90 g	12 oz	350 g
3½ oz	100 g	13 oz	375 g
4 oz	125 g	14 oz	400 g
5 oz	150 g	15 oz	450 g
6 oz	175 g	1 lb	500 g

INDEX

ABOUT THE AUTHOR

Leanne Brown is a very silly person who lives in New York City with her husband, Dan Lazin. She grew up in Edmonton, Canada, where her awesome family and many of her favorite people still reside. Before she moved to NYC, she liked to ride her bicycle everywhere. Now she rides sometimes, but takes the subway or walks other times. She likes to run in the park until she is really tired, eat pastries on the street, and go to bed late. She loves fairness, sci-fi and fantasy, tasty food, and laughing. She has been delighted by cooking and baking ever since she realized that they are the closest things we have to magic.

ACKNOWLEDGMENTS

First, special thanks to my husband, Dan. Your support and expertise were critical. But thank you most of all for never letting me give up or give in, even when I really wanted to. You make me a better person and without you, *Good and Cheap* would be just a shadow of what it is.

Thank you to Mum, Dad, Emily, Hannah, and Papa for your unconditional love and support. Thank you to my incredible friends who believed in this idea before anyone else. Your excitement was infectious! Your advice and support kept me sane. Thanks particularly to Jhen for jumping in, Claire for making me look good, and Sarah and Matt for making me feel powerful.

Thanks to my exceptionally patient and understanding editor, Liz, a great advocate and friend. And to Selina, John, Suzie, Jenny, Emily, Janet, Gordon, Orlando, and Amanda, who have given and continue to give so much to make this project a success, I cannot thank you enough. To everyone at Workman: Thank you for taking a chance with me. I'm positive that no other first-time author has ever benefitted from so much devotion from her publisher.

And thanks to all of you who shared your food stories: joyful, painful, incredible. You remind me every day why this work is important. The outpouring of love and support I've received is enough for several lifetimes, and I couldn't be more grateful. To those who told me this book has given them hope, inspired them, or otherwise brought them pleasure: I don't deserve so much gratitude for so little, but doing work that matters is all I have ever wanted.